THE CRITICS DEBATE

General Editor: Michael Scott

The Critics Debate
General Editor: Michael Scott
Published titles:
Sons and Lovers Geoffrey Harvey
Bleak House Jeremy Hawthorn
The Canterbury Tales Alcuin Blamires
Tess of the d'Urbervilles Terence Wright
Hamlet Michael Hattaway
The Waste Land and Ash Wednesday
   Arnold P. Hinchliffe
Paradise Lost Margarita Stocker
King Lear Ann Thompson
Othello Peter Davison
The Winter's Tale Bill Overton
Gulliver's Travels Brian Tippett
Blake: Songs of Innocence & Experience
   David Lindsay
Measure for Measure T. F. Wharton
The Tempest David Daniell
Coriolanus Bruce King

Further titles are in preparation.

THE TEMPEST

David Daniell

HUMANITIES PRESS INTERNATIONAL, INC.
Atlantic Highlands, NJ

First published in 1989 in the United States of America
by Humanities Press International, Inc.,
Atlantic Highlands, NJ 07716

Library of Congress Cataloging-in-Publication Data
Daniell, David.
  The Tempest.
  (The Critics debate)
  1. Shakespeare, William, 1564–1616.   Tempest.
I. Title.   II. Series.
PR2833.D36   1989   822.3′3   88–32866
ISBN 0–391–03641–6
ISBN 0–391–03642–4 (pbk.)

Printed in Hong Kong

Contents

Part Two: Appraisal

Acknowledgements

The author and publishers wish to thank the following who have kindly given permission for the use of copyright material: Frank Kermode, for material from the Introduction to The Arden Shakespeare, *The Tempest*, first published in 1954, and quoted here from the edition of 1964: and A. D. Nuttall, for material from *Two Concepts of Allegory* (1967).

Every effort has been made to trace all the copyright holders but if any have been inadvertently overlooked the publishers will be pleased to make the necessary arrangement at the first opportunity.

For Andy

General Editor's Preface

OVER THE last few years the practice of literary criticism has become hotly debated. Methods developed earlier in the century and before have been attacked and the word "crisis" has been drawn upon to describe the present condition of English Studies. That such a debate is taking place is a sign of the subject discipline's health. Some would hold that the situation necessitates a radical alternative approach which naturally implies a "crisis situation." Others would respond that to employ such terms is to precipitate or construct a false position. The debate continues but it is not the first. "New Criticism" acquired its title because it attempted something fresh, calling into question certain practices of the past. Yet the practices it attacked were not entirely lost or negated by the new critics. One factor becomes clear: English Studies is a pluralistic discipline.

What are students coming to advanced work in English for the first time to make of all this debate and controversy? They are in danger of being overwhelmed by the cross-currents of critical approaches as they take up their study of literature. The purpose of this series is to help delineate various critical approaches to specific literary texts. Its authors are from a variety of critical schools and have approached their task in a flexible manner. Their aim is to help the reader come to terms with the variety of criticism and to introduce him or her to further reading on the subject and to a fuller evaluation of a particular text by illustrating the way it has been approached in a number of contexts. In the first part of the book a critical survey is given of some of the major ways the text has been appraised. This is done sometimes in a thematic manner, sometimes according to various "schools" or "approaches." In the second part the authors provide their own appraisals of the text from their stated critical standpoint, allowing the reader the knowledge of their own particular approaches from which their views may in turn be evaluated. The series therein hopes to introduce and to elucidate criticism of authors and texts being studied and to encourage participation as the critics debate.

Michael Scott

Preface

UNIQUELY, *The Tempest* changes shape. Though it is well-printed, with few textual problems, and though its time of writing, and for what kind of audience, are facts now firmly established, what it 'means' seems to be continually on the move. It has always been a challenge, and never more than in the last years of the twentieth century.

The *Sea Venture* was wrecked on the Bermudas in a fearful storm in July 1609: accounts of that seem to have given Shakespeare some of the frame of his play. The wreck was discovered in the late 1970s: it lacked the timbers that were used by the castaways to make the smaller boat, the *Deliverance*, in which they continued to Virginia. At the end of Shakespeare's play, Ariel magically restores the wrecked ship. The Boatswain and crew find it 'tight and yare and bravely rigged, as when/We first put out to sea'. At the sight of 'our royal, good, and gallant ship' so restored, they see 'our master/Cap'ring to eye her' – a marvellously expressive phrase [v.i. 224–5. 237–8]. The company, without Ariel or Caliban, then sail on to Naples. Though the modern critic may dance for joy at the sight of the play – and indeed, should, or has no business writing about it – no such firm closure is possible; critically there is nothing so final as a sailing-away, either in a *Deliverance* or King Alonso's ship, to fix on. Ariel seems still at work, and the best that can be managed is perhaps a brief waking, and the recording of a few notes of the invisible music, as we all follow amazedly.

I have done what I could to give some shape – I hope not illusory – to the forces at work in this particular debate. The strongest voices have spoken in the last few decades, but a larger historical alertness is essential. Little that came later makes sense without knowledge of how the dam burst for the Romantic poets, for whom the play was unusually important:

11

and how that flooding fertilised our most recent Caliban–
Prospero binary system, however remote this is now from 'the
characters of Shakespeare's plays'. So I have taken time to
set out, where it seemed necessary, some critical history.
Moreover, as I try to sketch in Part Two, we have a long way
to go in understanding the creative, indeed 'civilising', quality
of *The Tempest*, from the court of James until now.

The play has been particularly blessed in its modern editors
(no doubt a further demonstration of Ariel still at work). One
edition, the Arden by Frank Kermode, first published in 1954
and continually reissued, is outstanding, and all writers on
the play since then have rightly acknowledged it. Anne
Barton's 1968 Penguin and Stephen Orgel's 1987 Oxford
editions are both excellent. Serious students should know all
three.

Quotations and references in what follows are from Peter
Alexander's one-volume *William Shakespeare: The Complete
Works*, first published in 1951.

Part One
Survey

THE TEMPEST IS the play which opens the great 1623 Folio of Shakespeare's works, and thus stands first in almost everybody's complete Shakespeare. It was the last complete play he wrote, in 1611. It is a strange, haunting, dream-like play full of wonderful poetry. It seems also to be full of puzzles.

1 Genres

Not least among the puzzles is what sort of a play *The Tempest* is. Since the general chronology of the plays was established, just over a hundred years ago, the last four – *Pericles* (1608), *Cymbeline* (1609), *The Winter's Tale* (1610), and *The Tempest* – have been lumped together as Romances, or Last Plays, or Late Comedies, or whatever. The Folio knows nothing of this: *Cymbeline* closes the Tragedies, *The Winter's Tale* closes the Comedies. *The Tempest* stands at the head of the Comedies. *Pericles* is omitted altogether. The divisions into Comedies, Histories or Tragedies made by the compilers of the Folio cannot be taken to be absolute. For one thing, there is, as Polonius indicated, a certain fatuousness in trying to pin down the right genre in the drama of the time ('tragedy, comedy, history, pastoral, pastoral-comical, historical-pastoral, tragi-cal-historical, tragical-comical-historical-pastoral' [*Hamlet*, II.ii.392–5]). Renaissance 'kinds' by the time of Shakespeare's last plays had become more mixed than ever (Colie 1973). For another, the Folio is not consistent: among the tragedies is '*The Life and death of Julius Caesar*', the formula used for three of the histories, including *Richard the Second*, which in Quarto is a '*Tragedy*'. Nevertheless, the effort of searching out the genre is worthwhile. Those four 'Romances' seem so very different from what he wrote before, in the meagreness of character-development, the fantastication of plots, and the new density of language; and Shakespeare appears to switch tracks so abruptly after the great tragedies (especially the sequence *Othello, King Lear, Macbeth, Antony and Cleopatra, Coriolanus* (1604–8)) that we do need to try to work out what he might be doing.

In fact, of course, we should always think not of his last four plays like that but of his last seven, including *King Henry the Eighth* (1612) which closes the histories, *Two Noble Kinsmen* (1612, not in Folio), and the mysterious *Cardenio*, of which only faint traces remain. Those three plays were written, it seems, in collaboration with John Fletcher. He, as the back half of the well-connected playwriting tandem we call 'Beaumont-and-Fletcher', specialised in a kind of romantic tragicomedy which appealed to the more exclusive audiences of the smaller, indoor, upstairs, Blackfriars Theatre. Beaumont and Fletcher wrote together from 1608, for a good while only for Shakespeare's company, the King's Men: it may well be that Shakespeare and his company, able in 1608 to move into the Blackfriars (which they had acquired in 1598) as a second house to the Globe, worked with Beaumont, and Fletcher, to produce a new kind of play (Bentley 1948).

In other words, we may do best to think of *The Tempest* as one of seven plays which, towards the end of his working life, Shakespeare wrote either alone, or in collaboration. In other words, again, *The Tempest*, though the last complete play he wrote, may come in the middle of a larger movement to something quite new. We can only guess at what made him move from tragedy so startlingly. The artistic jump seems both enormous and disturbing because, as Philip Edwards points out, it 'appears to be a change away from the control and concentration which Shakespeare had achieved in the great tragedies' (1958, p. 1). We can find links between the tragedies and the final seven, of course: Shakespeare's life-long interest in the ruler who leaves his responsibility is seen in King Lear, Antony, Coriolanus, Leontes in *The Winter's Tale* and Prospero in *The Tempest*. There are many other echoes. But from *Pericles* in 1608 Shakespeare's plays are quite different in kind.

What is that kind? And why did John Heminges and Henry

Condell, when making the copy for the Folio, and William and Isaac Jaggard when printing it, put *The Tempest* first? Perhaps it was still well enough known after its first performances, a dozen years before, to attract buyers. In their one-page preface, Heminges and Condell write 'whatever you do, buy'. The copy of *The Tempest* that the Jaggards printed seems to have been specially prepared to make it attractive to readers – the stage directions are uniquely full and literary, as if to help readers use their imaginations, rather than entirely to indicate to actors and stage-staff some essential action.

> *Enter certain* Reapers, *properly habited; they join with the Nymphs in a graceful dance; towards the end whereof Prospero starts suddenly, and speaks; after which, to a strange, hollow, and confused noise, they heavily vanish.*
>
> [IV.i.138.SD.]

What sort of play would have especially appealed to readers in 1623? In the late twentieth century, the more that critics look at *The Tempest*, the more difficulty they have in deciding what it is. Gary Schmidgall writes: 'The possibilities are admittedly boggling: *The Tempest* as romance, morality play, initiation ritual, refinement of the *commedia dell'arte*, topical response to New World voyages, masque, comedy, tragedy, tragicomedy, hymeneal celebration, fairy tale, myth, or autobiographical palinode' (1981, p. xv). And, he might have added, a set of magical devices, or a revenge play. I want here to show the main headings in the debate about genre, using categories that a reader in Shakespeare's time would have recognised.

Romance

The word was first applied to Shakespeare's four last plays by Dowden in 1875. It is a little more explicit than 'late plays', but it has the disadvantage of seeming to drain all Shakespeare's interest in Romance into his last work, which is unfair to a great deal that went before – many comedies, for example, and specifically the early *Comedy of Errors*, and *As You Like It* and *All's Well that Ends Well* in the middle of his career; parts of some tragedies; and even, it has been argued, the early *Richard the Third* (Kastan 1977). In these last plays, however, are lost royal children of unimpeachable virtue and beauty, final reconciliations and harmonies, escapes from death, artifices pointing to human fragility, adventures on, over or beside the sea – the very stuff of Romance. The form, as people under 'Eliza and our James' enjoyed it, came originally from ancient Greek prose stories, full-blooded tales of the marvellous, focused on young lovers, and on a wide canvas of seas and forests and mountains, with a long time-span, elemental disasters, improbable events, large adventures, disguises, supernatural interventions, heroic deeds, and final restorations. The form can be recognised more easily than it can be defined. Greek romance took many forms: *The Odyssey* itself fed largely into that ocean; Longus's *Daphnis and Chloe* of the second century AD is the best-known (Beer 1970; Gesner 1970; Dean 1979). Both Greek and medieval romances influenced Elizabethans, who relished Sidney's *Arcadia*, Spenser's *Faerie Queene*, the prose fictions of Greene and Lyly, and much, much else. Recent criticism has done well to show Shakespeare not only at home in the genre all his working life, but characteristically making something new of it (Pettet 1949; Wells 1966; Foakes 1971; Felperin 1972; White 1985). Howard Felperin, indeed, shows interestingly that Romance is both the genre and the subject of *The Tempest*: the play has both the open-endedness and idealisation of Romance, and at the same time a more rigorous pull towards closure – nothing so trite as a 'romantic' happy ending; rather an emphasis on the everyday reality of change. Quite what was the relation of Shakespeare's last plays to the Blackfriars Theatre is a matter of discussion. Bentley (1948) provoked challenge (Edwards 1958, 1973), particularly on the important grounds that in fact we know almost nothing about what happened, and the evidence is itself very small (Seltzer 1966). In 1611, Simon Forman saw *The Winter's Tale* at the Globe, and *Cymbeline* on an unknown date in an unstated theatre. A strong line of scholarship follows the activities of the King's Men in the period, giving some light on the problem (Proudfoot 1966; Sturgess 1987). But we are still to a great extent left speculating on the meaning of Romance for Shakespeare and his company (Hillman 1986).

Neo-classical drama

The last person to have appreciated Shakespeare's Romances would have been Ben Jonson, Shakespeare's first major critic. In his poem printed at the beginning of the First Folio, only seven years after Shakespeare's death, Jonson was at pains to point out Shakespeare's failure to use the correct neo-classical principles. This is part of what he is suggesting in his famous remark that Shakespeare had 'small Latin, and less Greek'. In fact, Shakespeare's knowledge of Latin was rather good (Binns 1982): Jonson was judging by his own superior classicising standard. He commended Shakespeare for having a lot of 'Nature', and then grudgingly noted only some 'Art': 'Yet must I not give Nature all; Thy Art/My gentle Shakespeare, must enjoy a part'. Though Jonson went on in these verses to commend Shakespeare's anvil-work, the accusation – for that is effectively what it was – was standard until Coleridge in 1809. Shakespeare had a 'natural' genius. He was full of 'faults' because of his ignorance of the correct way. Jonson expressed his dislike of Shakespeare's romance in the Prologue to his *Every Man in his Humour*, the Preface to *The Alchemist*, the Induction to *Bartholomew Fair*, and in the 'ode' appended to *The New Inn* – 'this mixture of abuse, snobbery, and bluster', as Felperin comments,

> is a fair summary of the defining features of Shakespearean romance: its archaism, its spatial and temporal sprawl, its fondness for music, dance, and spectacle, and especially, its inclusion of nonnatural elements and reliance on nonnaturalistic techniques of presentation. Underlying Jonson's animadversions on all these counts are the critical premises and prejudices later to surface in most of the neo-classical attacks on the romances from Dryden to Bernard Shaw.
>
> (1972, p. 291)

Yet we can now see *The Tempest* as Shakespeare's most neo-classical play. It is short, by the standards of the time, without signs of cutting. The stage-time matches the action – everything takes place on one sea-haunted afternoon. The place remains the same – patches of ground on a tropical island. There is effectively no subplot. These three 'unities' of time, place and action were increasingly said to be essential to making a drama: Aristotle was misrepresented as having said so, and neo-classical authors such as Jonson in England, and Corneille, Racine and Molière in France, certainly got remarkable effects from such restriction. Though it never really bit very deeply into our native drama, the scheme was discussed, and to some extent practised, for several centuries in England. (Indeed, Mr Curdle, in chapter 24 of Dickens's *Nicholas Nickleby* (1839), asks the hero about his play: 'I hope you have preserved the unities, sir? . . .The unities of the drama, before everything. . . . The unities, sir, are . . . a completeness – a kind of universal dovetailedness with regard to place and time, – a sort of general oneness, if I may be allowed to use so strong an expression.' In the same chapter, incidentally, is a splendid account of a melodramatic romance as put on by Mr Vincent Crummles's touring company at Portsmouth.) The unities make for intensive rather than extensive plays, never quite what has been generally thought 'Shakespearean'. But Shakespeare had used the unities twenty years before at the start of his career, in the only play shorter than *The Tempest, The Comedy of Errors*. That, too, is a sea-filled play about separation, but it was heavily based on Roman plays, and Plautus in particular. *The Tempest* has no model, and there, moreover, 'the unities of time and place are observed more stringently than any formulation demands' (William 1971, p. 435). R. S. White notes that 'the classical control and allusiveness are at their most prominent in the scene which is the most magical of all, the marriage masque created by Prospero's spirits' (1985, p. 159). Daniel C. Bougher (1970) shows that in *The Tempest* Shakespeare followed Jonson not only in observing such neo-classical unities, but in manipulating the four-part structure invented by Terence and described by Donatus, that of *prologue, protasis, epitasis* and *catastrophe:* it makes for movement from fear to hope, from anxiety to joy, and from revenge to forgiveness. That formula was revived by Machiavelli and given critical formulation by Scaliger: then adapted by Jonson for the English stage in *Every Man in His Humour* (1601) and *Epicoene* (1609). There is a case for seeing in *The Tempest* a sharply divided five-act structure (Brown 1969), and a classically rigorous form. Further, Harry Levin notes that: 'The conjunction of Jonson and Shakespeare was never closer or more productive than in the successive seasons of 1610 and 1611, when His Majesty's Servants introduced *The Alchemist* and *The Tempest* respectively.' Heading the actors' list for *The Alchemist* was Richard Burbage, who probably created 'Jonson's criminal master-mind and Shakespeare's wonder-working sorcerer' (Levin 1969). And Keith Sturgess remarks, 'A Blackfriars audience at *The Tempest* would not only see a Burbage–Lear–Prospero stage figure but also a Burbage–Subtle–Prospero stage figure' (Sturgess 1987, p. 76). There seems scope for more investigation here. Perhaps Jonson saw more classicism ('Art') in Shakespeare than he has usually been allowed to find. Bernard Knox, indeed (1954), finds *The Tempest* 'the most rigidly traditional of all Shakespeare's comedies except *The Comedy of Errors*' which has, of course, its own particular links with Plautus, Terence and Menander): and the most influential edition of *The Tempest*, Frank Kermode's Arden of 1954, gives full attention to the neo-classicism, both in design of the plot and the philosophical interests associated with that.

Masque

Certainly Jonson would have revelled in the masque elements in Shakespeare's play. Jonson was King James's chief provider of court masques, in rivalry with Inigo Jones as to who was paramount in the activity, poet or designer. There is a tradition that, like *A Midsummer Night's Dream, The Tempest* contains, or was itself, a court masque. Most recently, critics have found grounds for disagreement (Orgel 1987). The short dramatic entertainments called masques were mixtures of ingredients – poetry, dancing, music including songs, elaborate spectacle including gorgeous costumes, scenery and machines, clever lighting, and profoundly symbolic arrangements. These were acted by a mix of courtiers and professional actors. James, far more than Elizabeth, spent vast amounts of money on them, and made them important at court rather than on progresses out of London. Jonson perfected the art. Masque was a fluid genre, with no absolute lines between a dramatic performance and a revel. By the time of Shakespeare's last plays, even a less formal distinction between masque and drama was becoming harder to see, as the plays of Beaumont and Fletcher – for example, their *Four Plays or Moral Represen-*

tations in One – or Peele's *Arraignment of Paris*, or Jonson's *Cynthia's Revels*, show. Masque was paradoxical: 'it was exclusive and aristocratic, yet popular; it was artificial and sophisticated, yet primitive.' (Welsford 1927).

Now, the earliest comment we have on *The Tempest* must be the king's command performance at court, to take place in the Banqueting House at Whitehall on 1 November 1611, Hallowmass or All Saint's Day – and thus opening the winter season of court entertainments. It had probably played at the Blackfriars and the Globe before that, but at the Banqueting House it would go well in the hall so often fitted up for court masques, with machinery for transformation scenes, flying chariots, clouds and so on, and the tradition of inserted dances, in which the heir to the throne, Prince Henry, was outstandingly skilful: *The Tempest* has several formal dances, by 'strange shapes' [III.iii.17,82], and water-nymphs and reapers [IV.i.138]. Among other features, a banquet, 'with a quaint device . . . vanishes' [III.iii.52], and *Juno descends*. No Shakespeare play is so full of music. And so on. We know that in late October ten men spent six days preparing the Banqueting House for the performance, first, of a now unknown play, and then *The Tempest* the following night, and *The Winter's Tale* four days later: the King's Men, Shakespeare's company, led the theatrical activity at court. Though Inigo Jones was not involved, it is probable that the first performance of *The Tempest* was spectacular and masque-like – the betrothal-masque in IV.i and the banquet in III.iii would work well: and the scene of Caliban, Trinculo and Stephano being chased by 'divers Spirits, in shape of dogs and hounds' [IV.i.253] could be thought of as a variation on the anti-masque, an ingredient which Jonson had invented, in which lower elements set up discord which the courtly presences could then harmonise. 'Lower elements' might be from the audience, flattered to be included: but the 'courtly presences', both professional and elaborate, would celebrate the ideal rule – that is, of King James. It has long been thought that Jonson's court wedding masque, *Hymenaei*, of 1606, could well have contributed to Shakespeare's thinking about *The Tempest*: indeed, it is now suggested that he might have built his dramatic structure on the principle taught there – that of the Pythagorean canon of harmonic proportion (Orrell 1978). And Stephen Orgel suggests that the origin of Jonson's own development in pastoral masques between 1615 and 1620 could only have been learned from the masque of Ceres, Iris and Juno in *The Tempest* (1987).

Yet *The Tempest* itself is not a masque. It contains one, certainly, in iv.i, but neither that, nor the whole, is really a court masque. Frank Kermode wrote, of the other striking scene, iii.iii, that it is 'Shakespeare's most elaborate experiment in stage spectacle' (1964, p. 155) – which does not, of course, make it a masque. Some of the complexity of the betrothal masque is caught in E. M. W. Tillyard's remark that 'on the actual stage the Masque is executed by players pretending to be spirits, pretending to be real actors, pretending to be supposed goddesses and rustics' (1938, p. 80). There are masque-like complexities, indeed; but the whole play is not a masque. Earlier critics speculated, on no real evidence, that the play as we have it in Folio is a revision, with the iv.i masque as a special addition made for the court. A year after the first Banqueting House performance, during the winter of 1612–13, *The Tempest* was one of fourteen plays, several by Shakespeare, which the King's Men performed at court as part of the entertainment provided for the wedding of the king's daughter Princess Elizabeth to the Elector Palatine, Prince Frederick of Bohemia, on 14 February 1613. E. K. Chambers summarised the evidence but magisterially doubted revision (1930, i, p. 492; and 1944). Frank Kermode finally disposed of the suggestion (1964, pp. xvii–xxiv). More recently, Robert Grudin (1972) has a brief, philosophical essay showing how the masque is structurally related to the whole play. Further, David Lindley, examining *The Tempest*'s recurrent pattern of disrupted shows and its uneasy ending, finds Shakespeare sceptical about the power of the masque to change an audience: 'the Platonic theories that sustain a Sidneyan belief in art's golden world are crumbling, but we are left "wishing it might be so"' (1984, p. 58). It may be that there are more contradictions to explore.

Emblematic representation

Certainly, work remains to be done in the complex iconography of the play, and its use of emblems. 'The visual art of

Elizabethan England was a strange mingling of the schematic and the symbolic with the realistic', writes A. D. Nuttall. 'There was in those days a greater profusion of basic iconic symbols everywhere . . . not exhausted by heraldry and literary emblems. . . . The world of visual arts was, save at its most sophisticated levels, utterly dominated by the schematic and the symbolic' (1967, p. 77). The Magician figure, the Ariel spirit, the Virgin, the 'salvage and deformed slave', the island, the storm: such 'icons' are not so meaningful to us as when seen through a Jacobean filter. A. D. Nuttall, again, writes:

> Part of the process of learning to look at pictures of an earlier age consists in un-learning the conventions of one's own time, and in particular the convention of the one-one relationship whereby the representations of painters are more closely assimilated to the visual field. Thus one ceases to marvel at the fact that Cimabue apparently thought that the prophets were a set of identical quadruplets, and begins to realize that the faces of the prophets are not faces of individuals at all: they are old-men-and-nothing-else. (1967, p. 74)

The storm in the play has been linked by John Doebler (1974) to Giorgione's by then century-old painting, *Tempesta*, in an attempt to broaden the suggestiveness of the Renaissance readings of a storm, relating it too to a line from Pope's *Essay on Man* of 1733, 'The rising tempest puts in act the soul' (II. 105). In a similar way, Doebler hopes to open up the banquet in *The Tempest* (III.iii), seeing it as something effected by despair. 'Despair as the opposite psychological extreme to fortitude represents in this play a danger far greater than assassination, or the sea, or the punishment of Alonso and his companions by a revengeful Prospero' (pp. 149–50). In this context he sees an 'abbreviated Banquet of Sense' with all the Renaissance associations of betrayal and prodigality – both significances drawn out of the gospels – and of sin, especially greed, the particular attribute, he notes, of harpies. Prospero's hope is to use Ariel to bring Alonso to despair, and therefore repentance. Ariel's function at this point he finds to be dizzyingly complex; the significance of the magic circle which Prospero draws in the last act he makes even more so.

Such illumination can be helpful, as in Dieter Mehl's article 'Emblematic Theatre' (1977). Iconography, as a critical discipline, comes in and out of fashion rather rapidly: its history over the last decades is summed up in the notes to the first chapter of Ann Pasternak Slater's *Shakespeare the Director* (1982). There is room for more work on it in relation to *The Tempest*. Brian Loughrey and Neil Taylor have examined Ferdinand and Miranda at chess, finding the chess-board to be part of a play-within-the-play-within-the-play (1982). Rosemary Wright (1984) has discovered that Prospero's lime-tree at iv.i.193 is descended from emblems of the tree of knowledge, with significances of temptation, or mocking imitation, and of the 'late Gothic device of the pedlar and the apes'.

Commedia dell'Arte

Also awaiting reawakening is the idea which appealed to critics before the Second World War, that the striking resemblances between certain elements of the Italian popular comedy and *The Tempest* were more than coincidence. The *commedia* used 'typed and masked characters who improvised their parts from skeleton plots, which are called *scenari*, . . . [which] contain everything the trained extemporizer needed to get the plot along; and among those which are extant there are a few which are reminiscent of *The Tempest*' (Kermode 1964, p. lxvii). Some Italian players were in England quite late in the sixteenth century, and possibly again in 1610: and reports from Italy came back. Jonson used some of their devices. It seems an intriguing track to follow, and enthusiastic critics made a good deal of such things as the parallels between Italian comedy and the tricks of Stephano and Trinculo (Lea 1934). Kermode is almost too Johnsonian in dismissing the connection: 'he did not need a jocose pantomime to teach him how to think' (1964, p. lxviii). We do not have to go to Italy, however, to find a form of drama which was undoubtedly suggestive in the making of Shakespeare's romances.

Morality plays

Howard Felperin may stand for a group of critics who see *The*

Tempest as a secularised religious drama: not a miracle play –
though Sebastian refers to one with his 'A most high miracle!'
[v.i.177], about the Providential conclusion of the drama of
Alonso's family – but something more like a morality play,
the Tudor secular version of the medieval 'mystery' plays.
Those were accounts of the great Biblical events put on
by the guilds. That there are morality plays buried in
Shakespeare's romances, including *The Tempest*, has been
understood for some time: just as the medieval miracle play
can be seen as a version of a Greek romance, so the medieval,
chivalric romance can be seen to come from the same place
as the later morality plays (Hunter 1965). Felperin writes:

> In his appropriation and secularization of the forms of the medieval
> religious drama for his final romances, Shakespeare reassigns the role
> once played by the grace of God to the art of man: the role of raising
> and reforming mere nature. In the romances art is still closely associated
> with grace. But just as the private imaginative visions of Gonzalo,
> Antonio, and Caliban all fade before Prospero's higher and more
> comprehensive vision, so too, it is strongly hinted, Prospero's own vision
> fades before that of God. (1972, p. 278)

The brave new world of the end of the play is more substantial
than that implied by Prospero's earlier speech about the
ending of the revels. Prospero's vision was dispelled because
he had literally forgotten 'that hunk of brute nature that
Prospero has to "acknowledge" in the end but cannot reform'
(p. 279). Antonio, too, refuses reformation. And Prospero has
also to repudiate his 'dark and prideful learning' as Felperin
calls it (p. 276), and return to the ranks of humanity.

Pastoral

The setting of some of the action of *The Tempest* seems to make
it appropriate for a pastoral comedy. Shakespeare, writing
comedies, had always shown an interest in this idea – it is
originally Greek, and overlaps with Romance. From Theocri-
tus and Virgil, and from a romance like Longus's *Daphnis and
Chloe*, comes the developing notion that the pressures and
cynicisms of urban, and court, life, can be eased by going into
the country and leading an idealised existence as a shepherd,

doing little but be amorous in the sunshine and sing occasionally (Virgil took the form more seriously). Renaissance writers – Tasso, Sidney, Spenser – carried the suggestion forward. Playwrights of the late sixteenth and early seventeenth centuries seized the opportunities pastoral made for many layers of comment. Thus the principal court in *As You Like It* finds in the forest of Arden 'tongues in trees, books in the running brooks/Sermons in stones, and good in everything' [ii.i.16–17] – but that court is in forced exile. The young men who play at shepherds, buying 'the cottage, pasture, and the flock' [ii.iv.87] are really aristocratic young women in love – and played on the stage by young men. Meanwhile, the 'real' shepherds are lost in aristocratic, literary fictions of love. And so on. Moreover, what seems ideal in the soft noon airs of a Greek hillside in spring will not do at all on a wet winter's night in the English midlands: Duke Senior's rural court is perhaps a little over-hearty. But in Shakespeare's romances, pastoral dreams come to something else. Rurality in *Cymbeline*, and especially in *The Winter's Tale*, is a strong force for good. Not surprisingly, then, critics have found Prospero's island to be a pastoral retreat. By getting the wicked court party to experience an event in the country for a few hours, it is said, Prospero can try to win them to a new attitude. This endeavour is, like all Renaissance pastoral, utterly far-fetched and enchanting. *The Tempest* does in fact fit the pattern rather well, even to the conflict of views of the idealness of the landscape [*Tempest* ii.i – compare Touchstone's 'now am I in Arden; the more fool I', *As You Like It* ii.iv.12]. There is a hidden princess, there are fawning local fauna and a transformation indeed wrought by rural solitude, and the rest (Gesner 1970; McFarland 1972; Young 1972; Cody 1969).

Tragedy or comedy

The Tempest is the play which leads the comedies in Folio. Down the years, flocks of critics have happily labelled it a joyful comedy, and few have had the perception of Bonamy Dobrée that it is both shimmering and chill (1952). A surprisingly strong critical arm, however, particularly in the last two decades, reaches out to grasp this play as something close to out-and-out tragedy. D. G. James finds not only the possibility but the inevitability of tragedy (1967). Stephen Orgel finds the origin and the authority of the redemptive action of the play in the experience of tragedy. Prospero uses his art to shift perspectives: he does not deny tragedy – the characters are led through suffering to reconciliation – but transforms it. The ending includes the tragic implications of human nature (1962). We might label Jan Kott's dark vision of the play in his *Shakespeare Our Contemporary* (1965) not so much tragic as brutalist. The island is the stage whereon is enacted elementally the history of the world with its endless struggles for power. Prospero has usurped Caliban's island, as Antonio usurped Prospero's throne: the murder plotted by Sebastian, Antonio, and the 'foul conspiracy' re-enact a grim history. (The extraordinary influence of this perverse book, particularly in the United States of America, is something to wonder at. Intelligent readers are recommended to Patrick Cruttwell's 'Shakespeare is Not Our Contemporary' in *Yale Review*, 59, 1969.) There is, I am sure, a better case to be made for looking at *The Tempest* as a form of Revenge Tragedy. Deprive Prospero of his halo, and he does look like a powerful man driven by the need to avenge the great wrong he feels has been done to him: and the traditional delay of the form is all caught up in the recapitulation in i.ii. Now, at last, in his stage-managed play, Prospero has got everyone where he wants them, as in the last Act of a Revenge Tragedy, and he can take action. One does not have to look far to find the other traditional element, supernatural aids.

Pastoral tragicomedy

English drama has always been mixed in form. That is an over-simplified assessment, but just about defensible. To dip at random: in medieval Christian plays, the great and sometimes terrible Bible stories were told with some pagan gusto; Marlowe builds contrasting scenes; Webster at his darkest, flashes with wit. The greatest of Shakespeare's trage-dies have a comic element: the finest of his comedies contain most serious matter. This native stream, which has never dried up, had its fullest flood at the time of Elizabeth and James.

Sir Philip Sidney, in his *Apology for Poetry*, had in 1579 dismissed all 'mongrel' drama as unworthy of attention. By the time of Shakespeare's romances, however, new Italian ideas were in the London air. Samuel Daniel's *Queene's Arcadia*, 'a Pastoral Tragi-comedy', was performed in 1605. In 1608, John Fletcher produced, probably for the Blackfriars Theatre, even just possibly stimulated by Shakespeare's company, *The Faithful Shepherdess*, which brought directly to the London stage the theory and practice of the Italian critic Giambattista Guarini, whose *Compendio della Poesia Tragicomica* had been published in 1601. Guarini's book, and his play *Il Pastor Fido* of 1589, written to emulate Tasso, were important, and brought into English theatre life the Italian defence of tragicomedy as a genre, as well as a new strain of Italian pastoral drama. Fletcher modified Guarini's ideas slightly, but in his preface he discussed dramatic form directly in relation to Guarini. He wrote:

> A tragicomedy is not so called in respect of mirth and killing, but in respect it wants deaths, which is enough to make it no tragedy, yet brings some near it, which is enough to make it no comedy, which must be a representation of familiar people, with such kind of trouble as no life be questioned: so that a god is as lawful in this as in a tragedy, and mean people as in comedy. (Hirst 1984, pp. 12–13)

The new plays that Fletcher went on to write with Francis Beaumont, and the plays that Shakespeare wrote, alone or with Fletcher, and all probably for the Blackfriars, seem to be attempts to create Guarini's kind of tragicomedy, and often pastoral tragicomedy. The pastoral occupation is serious, dealing with the conflict of nature and nurture. David Hirst writes: 'The finest example of this new dramatic form is *The Tempest* which explores fundamental Shakespearean themes with a freshness and force resulting from a discipline akin to that advocated by Guarini' (Hirst p. 13). This understanding, that *The Tempest* is what Hirst calls 'a careful synthesis of elements from contrasted genres', has been most helpful. Shakespeare, he says 'combines the neo-classical techniques that enable him to effect a complete fusion of contrasted dramatic genres with his own profound understanding of human nature' (p. 33–4). Frank Kermode notes Guarini's position in a thirty-five-year controversy, affirming that pastoral was a moral and socially valuable genre, and that 'tragicomedy was critically acceptable provided it was not a clumsy intrusion of comedy into tragedy but a third kind, such as Aristotle allows for (*Poetics*, xiii), a harmonious mixture of comedy and tragedy and not a composite' (1964, p. lx, note). More work needs to be done on the Italian plays in the Guarini tradition. With a fresh look at the popular wing of the movement, the *commedia dell'arte*, a good deal on *The Tempest* could yet come to light. Though royal births, and resurrection from death, real or apparent, are in Guarini and Fletcher, Frank Kermode's words suggest a proper proportion for Shakespeare's plays:

> Even if we cannot ascertain its antecedents, there can be no question that the tragicomic form of the last plays was dictated by the nature of the fables treated, and that these were chosen because they lent themselves to the formulation of poetic propositions concerning the status of human life in relation to nature, and the mercy of a providence which gives new life when the old is scarred by sin or lost in folly. The themes are thus pastoral and tragicomic.   (1964, p. lxi)

These high matters will appear again in this study, when we come to modern understanding of the philosophies discovered to be at work in the play. To set such criticism in its place, I need to sketch here the critical reactions to the play from its earliest performances.

2 Characters

Critical history, 1611–1875

The history of responses to *The Tempest* is also the criticism of the comedies of Shakespeare, until the work of the Romantic poets in the early nineteenth century – with the unique exception that no play of Shakespeare, or indeed of anyone, has, from the time that it was written right up to the present day, stimulated such remarkable further works of art. This is something that I will take further in Part Two: for now we note that from Milton's *Comus* to Auden's *The Sea and The*

Mirror and beyond, poets (and not only poets) have found their own creative form of comment on the play.

The Tempest does not seem to have been among the most referred-to of Shakespeare's plays in its first half-century of life. There are considerably fewer allusions to it than to *Romeo and Juliet*, for example, and many fewer than to *Hamlet*. In the seventeenth and eighteenth centuries, it was understood that the critical agenda had been set by Ben Jonson, as we saw above, p. 17. In most early comments, Shakespeare is 'sweet' – Jonson calls him the 'sweet Swan of Avon' – and 'sugared', and 'honeyed' in various ways. (Some of these references, it is true, are to his Ovidian poems rather than to plays.) He is praised for his membership of, as Jonson said, 'Nature's family'. Milton caught it exactly in about 1631: 'If. . . sweetest Shakespeare, Fancy's child/Warble his native woodnotes wild'. Dryden, in the most important work of criticism of the century, his *Essay of Dramatic Poesy* (1668), wrote of Shakespeare:

> He was the man who of all modern, and perhaps ancient poets had the largest and most comprehensive soul. All the images of Nature were still present to him, and he drew not laboriously, but luckily; when he describes any thing, you more than see it, you feel it too. Those who accuse him to have wanted learning, give him the greater commendation; he was naturally learn'd; he needed not the spectacles of books to read Nature; he looked inwards, and found her there.

After the Restoration in 1660, and for well over a hundred years, his faults were said to have been the faults of the time: he had had the misfortune to have been writing in a barbaric age. Natural beauties, yes: but he is full of errors – jewels amid the rubbish, as critics at the end of the eighteenth century liked to put it.

The attention given to *The Tempest* before the Romantic critics in the early nineteenth century – which is not much – skirmishes on that border where Nature meets Art. Shakespeare needed correction for modern taste, and also absolutely, because he got it wrong: (Dryden in his *Essay* chose a Jonson play as the model because 'Shakespeare . . . did not perfectly observe the laws of Comedy'). Such correction was done in three main ways, as it still is. First is textual emendation. The received text may appear to be faulty: it may not make sense to 'modern' readers, or it may offend taste, so it has to be changed. In the eighteenth and nineteenth centuries, the Immortal Bard could not be permitted to use 'low' words, and enthusiastic or learned gentlemen announced what he should have written, with frequently comic results. The second method is the writing of a critical essay which points out both some matters for admiration, and the faults. Until the Romantics, that work tended to be closely linked with the preparation of an edition, though there were occasional free-standing comments. What notes there are on *The Tempest* tend to relate to Caliban, who acts as a sort of check-point at the border between Nature and Art. References are made to 'the Monster in the *Tempest*'. Thus Dryden, in his long preface to *Troilus and Cressida*, digresses to give an account of Shakespeare's mixture of Nature and Art in *The Tempest*. Shakespeare succeeded because he needed no book-learning, but only his poetic invention, his imagination. So Caliban is an entirely new species: 'he seems there to have created a person which was not in Nature, a boldness which at first sight would appear intolerable'. Caliban as the apogee of Shakespeare's untutored genius was appealed to again and again. There grew from that the notion that Shakespeare had even furnished Caliban with his own language, an idea which lived on until a growl from Samuel Johnson frightened it away in 1765.

It was, in fact, because of his supposed inadequacies that Shakespeare was not really touched by the great critical debate of the latter part of the seventeenth century, the Paris-based 'Battle of the Books', that quarrel between the Ancients and the Moderns so splendidly handled by Swift. Dryden in the *Essay* tried to use Shakespeare to score for the Moderns, but had to admit that his heart rather than his head was controlling him – 'I admire him [Jonson], but I love Shakespeare'.

The Caliban that Dryden characterised was sufficiently malevolent. This is not true of the 'Monster' who appeared in *The Tempest, or the Enchanted Island. A Comedy* by Dryden and Davenant in 1667. For the third method of correction was, as it still is, that of wholesale rewriting. We think of this, rightly, as being a habit of Restoration dramatists, though it is very much alive today. *The Tempest* has suffered this fate fairly regularly. But before *The Enchanted Island*, Dryden tells us, there were versions of *The Tempest* early in the century: *The*

Sea Voyage by John Fletcher, acted at the Globe in 1622; and *The Goblins* by Sir John Suckling (1638). Both plays were acted in the late 1660s. Neither play comes anywhere near *The Tempest*, apart from superficial similarities of island settings and sailors. Indeed, both plays vulgarise the idea of a beautiful young woman who has never seen a man, until . . . and so on. Dryden and Davenant's play was an even sorrier vulgarisation. It was one of the most successful of the Restoration Shakespeare adaptations, and was still performed to applause at the end of the eighteenth century: and itself in 1674 spawned an operatic version, which was even more successful, and in 1675 a farce. The adaptors keep less than a third of Shakespeare, and they are particularly self-satisfied about it. (Davenant liked to think of himself as a natural child, literally, of Shakespeare.) They try to restore what they think of as classical balance by giving Caliban a sister called Sycorax, Miranda a sister called Dorinda, and Ariel a fiancée. They introduce an important new character, a young man called Hippolito, a ward of Prospero and the rightful Duke of Mantua. He is found to be in special, and great, danger:

> PROSP.   O, gentle youth! fate waits for thee abroad,
>   A black star threatens thee, and death, unseen,
>   Stands ready to devour thee.
> HIP.   You taught me not to fear him in any of his shapes:
>   Let me meet death rather than be a prisoner.
> PROSP.   'Tis pity he should seize thy tender youth.
> HIP.   Sir, I have often heard you say, no creature lived
>   Within this isle, but those which man was lord of.
>   Why, then, should I fear?
> PROSP.   But here are creatures which I named not to thee,
>   Who share man's sovereignty by nature's laws,
>   And oft depose him from it.
> HIP.   What are those creatures, sir?
> PROSP.   Those dangerous enemies of man, called women.
> HIP.   Women! I never heard of them before.
>   What are women like?

Prospero tells him over the next thirty lines, apparently salivating.

This was the play Pepys saw, sitting high up in the Duke's

House (Davenant's own theatre) on 7 November 1667, its first performance. He sat 'close by my Lady Dorsett and a great many great ones: the house mighty full, the King and Court there, and the most innocent play that ever I saw. . . . The play no great wit, but yet good, above ordinary plays.' It is, to late-twentieth-century taste, a cheap and silly play, the radical surgery on Shakespeare's living flesh producing only a cripple. Yet it is faithful to Shakespeare by comparison to the appalling mayhem done to *Coriolanus* by Nahum Tate in 1682, or to many other Restoration reworkings of the comedies. (One of my own favourite moments is from Davenant's play *The Law against Lovers*, performed on 15 February 1662, a concoction which is *Measure for Measure* combined with *Much Ado About Nothing*, when in Act IV scene i *'Enter* Viola *dancing a Saraband awhile with Castanietos'*.)

Dryden and Davenant's play has been scorned: very recent critics have been bold, however, to see what it might represent as comment on Shakespeare. Dryden and Davenant's symmetrical doublings, matching Miranda who has never seen a man except her father not only with a similar sister, but with Hippolito who has never seen a woman, and so on, only extend something already in Shakespeare's *Tempest*, a structure of pairings and oppositions – the antithetical Ariel and Caliban, for example, or the two conspiracies against a sleeping victim (against Alonso, and against Prospero by Caliban), or the opposition of Prospero's white magic with Sycorax's black: these all invite comparison, and such comparison produces challenges to understanding (Brown 1960; Barton 1968; Maus 1982; Powell 1984; Orgel 1987)

The cultural climate began to change only a few years after Shakespeare's *Tempest* was written. So great was that change that after a hundred years, and far into the following century, Ben Jonson's apparent prejudice against Shakespeare as a writer whose abounding imagination was never properly checked by learning ('Shakespeare never blotted line. Would he had blotted a thousand') was being taken as gospel. Samuel Johnson in 1765 could not find anything good to say in his notes on *The Tempest*, dismissing, for example, Ariel's 'lays' as 'of no supernatural dignity or elegance'. He wrote that 'they express nothing great, nor reveal anything above mortal discovery' – it is astonishing to modern ears that he is referring

to 'Full fathom five' and the other songs. Even the rise of
Bardolatry, from the 1770s onwards, which exalted Shakespeare to the status of being not just the greatest Englishman,
but the greatest human being who ever lived, did not properly
shift the sense that he had had the greatest misfortune to live
in, and be corrupted by, such a grossly barbaric age. Elizabeth
Montagu wrote in 1769 that 'Shakespeare's plays were to be
acted in a paltry tavern, to an unlettered audience just
emerging from barbarity.' As Jonathan Bate writes, adapting
a remark by William Blake, 'To generalise about the eighteenth
century is to be an idiot' (Bate 1986, p. 6). True: but the
shock of the rediscovery of Shakespeare by the Romantic
poets, and that sense of liberation, show the comments in the
eighteenth century to be stuck, throughout the whole period
from the Restoration, in the same groove. Writers in the late
1790s could still berate Shakespeare for lack of both taste and
knowledge of the laws of drama.

Reading the criticism of Shakespeare by the Romantic poets
is to feel that a dam has burst, and the flood of Shakespearean
richness can now spread into every part of English poetry.
Indeed, the very understanding of Imagination itself, in the
new full Romantic sense, was pretty well defined by reference
to Shakespeare – and particularly in relation to *The Tempest*,
which now suddenly came into its own. It is the play most
commented on, after the 'imaginative Tragedies', *Hamlet, King
Lear* and *Macbeth*. The revolution begins with Coleridge in the
first decade of the nineteenth century, though whether he
learned from A. W. Schlegel or Schlegel learned from him has
been disputed. Coleridge's Shakespeare criticism comes to us
in bits and pieces, but it has been the most influential. His
criticism, stemming from new and organic, rather than old
and mechanical, principles, showed the importance of imagination for *The Tempest*. He established three general significances: that Shakespeare was indeed a great artist, whose form
is natural, shaping itself as it develops from within: and that
he was a great poet, a truth to which the eighteenth century
had seemed deaf. Coleridge's third point emerged from the
attention he gave to opening scenes and some *minutiae* within
them, which revealed Shakespearean drama as a unified
whole – the famous illustration is the 'single happy epithet'
crying in Prospero's account of his flight from Milan with the

infant Miranda [I.ii.132]. Prospero, indeed, now stood for the poet as Coleridge saw himself: the 'mighty wizard whose potent art could not only call up the spirits of the deep, but the characters as they were and are and will be, seems a portrait of the bard himself' (Raysor 1960, ii p. 135; ii p. 253). For Wordsworth, again, the poet is Prospero, whose 'Ye elves of hills, brooks, standing lakes, and groves' [v.i.33] opens up for him invocations to nature. Shakespeare was the presiding genius of Keats's maturing: the seven little volumes of Shakespeare which he took to the Isle of Wight in April 1817 show in their markings the plays that meant most, as well as his exasperation with Johnson's ponderous comments. *The Tempest* is one of the two plays most heavily marked and thumbed (*A Midsummer Night's Dream* is the other), and he saw his glimpse of 'negative capability' through Shakespeare. Behind Keats stood Hazlitt (or rather sat: Keats wrote in his copy of Hazlitt's *Characters of Shakespeare's Plays* 'I cannot help seeing Haslitt like Ferdinand – in an odd angle of the Isle sitting – his arms in this sad knot', Bate 1986, p. 262), particularly Hazlitt's enthusiasm for Shakespeare's impersonal artistic development. Shelley and Byron too were liberated Romantic Shakespeareans. The gift of Coleridge, Keats and Hazlitt to the world was a new Shakespeare, with a *Tempest* as particularly important. Now what shapes the design of the whole play is seen as a vision of character and plot, a triumph of the imagination rooted in deep intuitive understanding of human nature. Interpretation of the whole, from the grandest design to the smallest detail, is now possible.

For each of the Romantics, thinking about dream or earthly transience tended to call up *The Tempest* and Prospero and all his great speeches of strong imagination. This was wholly healthy. It was a subromantic experience of late Victorianism, which coincided with the establishing of the chronology of the final plays, which led to the shift from Prospero as Poet to Prospero as *The* Poet, i.e. Shakespeare. The Romantic sense of the soul of Shakespeare had taken form: a figure had emerged from the mist. Dowden (1875) could then famously write a spiritual autobiography of Shakespeare, and draw the portrait of a Final Period Shakespeare who wrote *The Tempest*, and the other Romances, as an idealised dream of contented old age.

We still, in criticism of *The Tempest*, breathe the air of Romantic thought: we still seek Shakespeare's soul.

Character studies

For Dowden, Shakespeare was himself a 'character', developing through his plays. Victorian monographs on the girlhood of Shakespeare's heroines or whatever, trying to turn the shadows into biographical reality, represented the vulgar wing of a movement to understand something important. Though Cambridge critics in the 1930s chose to deride A. C. Bradley, whose great *Shakespearean Tragedy* of 1904 was thought by them to treat the figures in the plays as if they were in a Victorian novel, critical studies of characters have been very much alive, and such work is still a flourishing industry. For generations of British schoolchildren, 'Shakespeare' in classrooms has meant the study of characters. 'Write an essay on the character of Mark Antony'; 'Contrast Brutus and Cassius as characters'; 'What contributes to the character of Prospero?'; 'What differences do you see between the characters of Perdita and Miranda?' Only slightly more sophisticated, late-twentieth-century academic critics, particularly in America, have tried to use the crafts of both Freudian psychoanalysis and Jungian analytic psychology in an attempt to get down into the murk below the surface, into the depths of Shakespeare's insights into human nature. Debate is vigorous.

Psychoanalytic studies

These have been led from the Freudian corner by the many publications by Norman N. Holland and Murray Schwartz, both from the Centre for the Psychological Study of the Arts at Buffalo, New York. From elsewhere come studies of *The Tempest*'s revelation of fantasies of 'the family romance', incestuous desires, death, narcissism, and so on. In late-twentieth-century psychoanalytic studies we seem a long way from the generally benign view of the play which dominated the nineteenth, though even in the middle of that century actors and critics were coming to recognise that there were difficulties with a wholly benevolent Prospero. Now, for example, Coppélia Kahn (1980) suggests that the brother Antonio stands for Prospero's absent father (who is the real usurper of the mother's kingdom); and Joel Fineman (1980) disagrees. David Sundelson 'centers on Shakespeare's drive toward an affirmative representation of fatherhood, and he sees the play as a study in paternal narcissism that depicts the father as the sole authority whose dominion shelters, nurtures, and even creates (in the numerous rebirths Prospero sponsors) everyone in the play' (Schwartz and Kahn 1980, p. xvii).

Yet there is something odd about a good deal of such psychoanalytic study, pointed out by Stephen Orgel:

> More even than *Hamlet*, the play tempts us to fill in its blanks, to create a history that will account for its action, and most of all for its hero. Indeed, recent psychoanalytic criticism has found in Prospero and in the conflicting wills around him a complex case history – though whose case history is a question that is dealt with less persuasively. Such readings probably testify, again, more to the play's ambivalences and ambiguities than to its psychological consistency. It offers to the psychologizing imagination primarily a world of possibilities, enormously suggestive, but incompletely realised and in significant respects unresolved. It is, indeed, in the matter of the play's resolution that psychological readings, and Freudian readings in particular, tend to have most difficulty accommodating themselves to the text. This is not surprising: if the critical model is a psychoanalytic one, the working out of problems will inevitably be its subject: and if the play is conceived as therapy, the analyst-critic will have a stake in a successful conclusion. In this respect, even very sophisticated Freudian readings tend to be romance readings, ultimately sentimental, emphasizing the promised resolution and ignoring the plays's unwillingness to fulfil it.   (1987, pp. 11–12)

I add only that the current American critical preference for the utterly positive can be, in fact, a matter of hard-nosed reality. The academic who chose to write about *The Tempest* as part of his own therapy would not further his career should he admit at the end of it that he found himself abandoned like Caliban. So he won't do it. In other words, this particular critical process is more obviously loaded from the start than most.

Jungian critics tend to see the plays of Shakespeare from a long way away. Like the court of Lilliput, the figures take on a fresh significance when seen through the wrong end of a telescope. Archetypes such as the Old Wise Man, and discussion of the *anima* and *animus*, can make comment on *The Tempest* seem profoundly significant. Alex Aronson is interesting, for example, in relating Prospero's brother Antonio to other brothers (Claudius in *Hamlet*, Edmund in *King Lear*) who represent a 'shadow'. Like much Jungian criticism, however, the writing aims to be compelling by means of the wide sweep of the arm: discussing Ophelia, for example (in a characteristic passage) he writes that 'this renewal pattern . . . must have lain dormant in Shakespeare's creative imagination when, at a later stage, he let Cordelia fulfil her fate as her father's anima, and created Miranda rising out of the water into which Ophelia had sunk, embodying a chastity consciously preserved and knowingly shared with her lover' (Aronson 1972, p. 180). Symbols rather than text take control, and detail is smudged. The Jungian process of individuation has some parallels with the movement of a drama towards resolution: but because each play, according to Jungian theory, can only have one possible centre of consciousness, it seems unlikely that this route into a play's unconscious is going to give much insight into the rich complexity which is a Shakespeare play. Frank Kermode sums up magisterially: 'Any reader who comes to this work ['C. G. Jung's *The Integration of the Personality*] with *The Tempest* in mind will see how rich it is in material for a Jungian interpretation, not only of the narrative part of the play, but also of the element of magic. But Shakespeare's is the High Dream of Dante, and not the psychic residua of the consulting room (Kermode 1964, p. lxxxiii, n.3).

Feminist readings

Barbara Melchiori wrote in 1960 an essay 'Still Harping on My Daughter', about incest in the late plays, which might stand for many critics' interest now, later in the twentieth century. It is a contrast with the Victorian sentimental imaginings about girlhood. Feminist criticism of *The Tempest*, mostly now American, concentrates on fathers and daughters, using rather homemade weapons constructed out of some of the ideas of Freud and Jung. Though Prospero and the fourteen-year-old Miranda seem ripe for such analysis, specifically feminist readings of *The Tempest* have not quite matched the statutre of feminist writing on the tragedies and earlier comedies. Indeed, almost all the feminist criticism of *The Tempest* that I have seen has been at a depressingly low standard. To restrict suggestions only to one part of the field, there is room for work on the mothers of Miranda and Caliban: the female figures in the play in the masque and elsewhere: the parallels between Ferdinand and Caliban as suitors for Miranda; and the sheer complexitiy of the relationship of Prospero and Miranda. Some of this is tackled in Stephen Orgel's 'Prospero's Wife' (Orgel 1984), though there the relationships in the play, and some observations of psychoanalysis, are used more to delineate and ponder on the play's characteristic absences (and Orgel does seem to me to be untypically imperceptive about, for example, married couples in Shakespeare's plays).

3 Themes

I shall discuss the more fully symbolic studies of the play later. Such criticism is concerned less with the interaction of characters, and more with supposed evidences of grander designs altogether, by means of various extensions of metaphor and allegory. It is important, before I do so, to separate the essential work done on the themes of the play in the last decades from those majestic symbolic illuminations which can so easily become the moonbeams of a larger lunacy. And even discussion of themes needs caution.

The comedienne Victoria Wood has a comic sketch about a 'paralytically nervous' schoolgirl attending an interview for a place in a British medical school. She is asked what was the last book she read, and she replies '*Othello*'. The first interviewer asks, 'What do you think is the main theme of *Othello*?' She replies, 'I don't think its got one, really. It's just various people talking, and sometimes they do things in brackets.' She is right, of course. Shakespeare wrote plays – people talking and doing things. There has grown up among critics not of the first rank the notion that plays are *about* 'themes'. Thus an American feminist wrote in 1984 that Shakespeare's plays are 'symbolic transformations of ambivalence about gender relations', going on to announce that *King Lear* is 'about the conflicts between distance and emotion in relations between parent and child'. A book which should be gift-wrapped and presented at the christening of every future critic is Richard Levin's *New Readings vs Old Plays* (1979). Levin, increasingly distressed by the eagerness of critics in America to assert abstract subject-matter, investigated the evidence for the way in which some 140 Tudor and Stuart plays were received at the time of first performance in London – that is to say, by the audiences for which they were written. He contrasts that evidence with the fancy modern 'readings': Thematic Readings, Ironic Readings, Historical Readings (pointing out the dangers of 'Ideas-of-the-Time') and the Occasionalist Scene, concluding with twenty vigorous pages quoting American critics' follies of 'Christ-figure' hunting. Early in this exhilarating book, on page 17, is the following imaginary dialogue, which Levin tries to picture taking place between Ben Jonson and William Shakespeare in a tavern on the Bankside:

B. J.   What have you been doing lately, Will?
W. S.   I've been working on a new play.
B. J.   Oh, what will it be about?
W. S.   It will be a sustained meditation on reality and illusion.

What James I and his court saw on All Saints Day 1611 was a play, not a farrago of modern jargon.

And yet: the king and his courtiers, attending a masque in the Banqueting House in Whitehall, would expect an outcome in which Virtue, Peace, Beauty, Harmony, Right Rule and so on, triumphed. Watching Shakespeare's *Tempest*, they would see a pastoral tragicomic romance, with masque elements. It is not only in order, it is essential, to discuss, in dealing with *The Tempest*, both the traditions of romance drama in England, and the special literary conventions of pastoral romance as they appear, for example, in Sidney's *Arcadia* and Spenser's *Faerie Queene*, and to know how the play shares themes within these conventions. One of the many ways in which Frank Kermode's Arden edition of *The Tempest* was important was that it first, and most lucidly, set out that:

The Tempest, though exceptionally subtle in its structure of ideas, and unique in its development of them, can be understood as a play of an established kind dealing with situations appropriate to that kind. *The Tempest* is a pastoral drama; it belongs to that literary kind which includes certain earlier English plays, but also, and more significantly, *Comus*; it is concerned with the opposition of Nature and Art, as serious pastoral poetry always is, and it shares this concern with the other late comedies, and with the Sixth Book of the *Faerie Queen*, to which it is possibly directly indebted.

The two following paragraphs must also be quoted in full:

The main opposition is between the worlds of Prospero's Art, and Caliban's Nature. Caliban is the core of the play; like the shepherd in formal pastoral, he is the natural man against whom the cultivated man is measured. But we are not offered a comparison between a primitive innocence in nature and a sophisticated decadence, any more than we are in *Comus*. Caliban represents (at present we must over-simplify) nature without benefit of nurture; Nature, as opposed to an Art which is man's power over the created world and over himself; nature divorced from grace, or the senses without the mind. He differs from Iago and Edmund in that he is a 'naturalist' by nature, without access to the art that makes love out of lust; the restraints of temperance he cannot, in his bestiality, know; to the beauty of the nurtured he opposes a monstrous ugliness; ignorant of gentleness and humanity, he is a savage and capable of all ill; he is born to slavery, not to freedom, of a vile and not of a noble union; and his parents represent an evil natural magic which is the antithesis of Prospero's benevolent Art.

This is a simple diagram of an exquisitely complex structure, but it may be useful as a guide. Caliban is the ground of the play. His function is to illuminate by contrast the world of art, nurture, civility: the world which none the less nourishes the malice of Antonio and the guilt of Alonso, and stains a divine beauty with the crimes of ambition and lust. There is the possibility of purgation; and the tragicomic theme of the play, the happy shipwreck – 'that which we accompt a punishment against evil is but a medicine against evil' – is the means to this end.   (pp. xxiv, xxv)

Nature

In the central 35 pages of his introduction, Kermode shows how the current voyage-literature, particularly the 1610 Bermuda pamphlets (see below pp. 70–5) 'seem to have precipitated, in this play, most of the major themes of Shakespeare's

last years: indeed, that is their whole importance'. He goes
on:

> The events of 1609 in Bermuda must have seemed to contain the whole
> situation in little. There a group of men were, as they themselves
> said, providentially cast away into a region of delicate and temperate
> fruitfulness, where Nature provided abundantly; brought out of the
> threatening but merciful sea into that New World where, said the
> voyagers, men lived in a state of nature. Ancient problems of poetry and
> philosophy were given an extraordinary actuality. (p. xxv)

Shakespeare, however, was careful to set his play in the Old
World, between Naples and Tunis: he was appealing to an
altogether wider set of significances. Kermode writes:

> The natural life, the Golden Age, and related themes, giving rise as they
> do to considerations of justice and mercy, man fallen and redeemed, the
> reclamation of nature by the ministers of grace – these themes are
> constantly heard in *The Tempest*; but although the complex in which they
> are heard is peculiar to the play, they were not novel to the contemporary
> reader of travel literature. (p. xxx).

That literature included the *Aeneid* (again, see below p. 88),
and the fabulous holy voyages of *The Golden Legend*, and
especially Montaigne, as far as his essay 'Of Cannibals' (in
Florio's translation, which Shakespeare used) can be called
travel literature. Montaigne seems to suggest that Natural
Men, in a primitive natural society, would be happy, and
offers the New World as an example of naturally virtuous life
uncorrupted by Civilisation. Shakespeare is sceptical. Both
sides of the debate – holding the primitive as Golden, or
vicious – found evidence in the narratives they studied.
At issue also was whether man's interference with Nature
corrupted, or was itself part of Nature – the very topic which
King Polixenes and Princess Perdita debate, importantly, in
The Winter's Tale [iv.iv.70–108]. So there were two versions of
the natural: 'that which man corrupts . . . and that which is
defective, and must be mended by civilisation. . . . This latter
is the view which suits best the conscience of the colonist'
(Kermode, p. xxxvi).

Prospero assumes, as a European prince, his right to rule
the island, 'to be the lord on't': the exploitation of the
inhabitants of fertile territory, something 'at once virtuous

and expedient', as Kermode puts it, has been the subject of very sharp recent discussion. (See below, pp. 77–81; for excellent additional material on the significance of travel literature to the play see Brockbank 1966; James 1967; Frey 1979.)

In *The Tempest*, Shakespeare uses Caliban partly to indicate how much baser the corrupt civilised world can be than the bestiality of the natural. In the play, nature is complex. Antonio and Sebastian jeer at Gonzalo's view of it. He is wrong, apparently, about some pretty basic things (but see below). Yet Gonzalo pronounces the benediction to the play, and Antonio and Sebastian prove incapable of alteration.

The key is Caliban:

> The poetic definition of Nature in the play is achieved largely by a series of antitheses with Caliban constantly recurring as one term. He represents the natural man. This figure is not, as in pastoral generally, a virtuous shepherd, but a salvage and deformed slave. (Kermode, p. xxxviii)

Kermode's equation of Caliban with a European wild man has been challenged recently, as I shall show. Unmistakably, however, Caliban is the necessarily deformed product of a sexual union between a witch and an incubus – evil natural magic, a natural criterion by which we measure the world of Art, represented by Prospero's divine magic and the supernaturally sanctioned beauty of Miranda and Ferdinand. (I say 'unmistakably', but as Stephen Orgel points out, we have only Prospero's word for this, he apparently having got it from Ariel. It is possible that it is 'an especially creative piece of invective' (Orgel 1984, p. 5)). Kermode writes:

> Caliban is, therefore, accurately described in the Folio 'Names of the Actors'. His origins and character are natural in the sense that they do not partake of grace, civility, and art; he is ugly in body, associated with an evil natural magic, and unqualified for rule or nurture. He exists at the simplest level of sensual pain and pleasure, as music can appeal to the beast who lacks reason; and indeed he resembles Aristotle's bestial man. He is a measure of the incredible superiority of the world of Art, but also a measure of its corruption. For the courtiers and their servants include the incontinent Stephano and the malicious Antonio. Caliban scorns the infirmity of purpose exhibited by the first, and knows better than Antonio that it is imprudent to resist grace, for which, he says, he will henceforth seek. . . . Men can abase their degree below the bestial;

and there is possibly a hint, for which there is no support in Aristotle, that the bestial Caliban gains a new spiritual dimension from his glimpse of the 'brave spirits'. Whether or not this is true, he is an extraordinarily powerful and comprehensive type of Nature; an inverted pastoral hero, against whom civility and the Art which improves nature may be measured. (Kermode pp. xlii–xliii)

Art

The courtiers have a fortunate seed within them, are of good stock, endowed with grace, and 'nurtured in refinement through the centuries in the world of Art' – though an evil disposition can inhere in good stock, as in Antonio. Prospero's art is both as mage, disciplining through learning and temperance, working towards harmony: and as a symbol of the control of Nature. 'Art is not only a beneficent magic in contrast to an evil one,' writes Kermode; 'it is the ordination of civility, the control of appetite, the transformation of nature by breeding and learning; it is even, in a sense, the means of Grace' (p. xlviii). Kermode further shows the advantage to Shakespeare of the forms he used –

> The romantic story is, then, the mode in which Shakespeare made his last poetic investigation into the supernatural elements in the human soul and in human society. His thinking is Platonic, though never schematic; and he had deliberately chosen the pastoral tragicomedy as the genre in which this inquiry is best pursued. The pastoral romance gave him the opportunity for a very complex comparison between the worlds of Art and Nature; and the tragicomic form enabled him to concentrate the whole story of apparent disaster, penitence, and forgiveness into one happy misfortune, controlled by a divine Art.
> (pp. lviii–lix)

This has rightly dominated work on *The Tempest* in the second half of the twentieth century: editors and major critics all acknowledge its importance.

The Tempest *as invitation*

The Tempest is unique in its open-ness, though that is part of

its nature as romance. *Hamlet* criticism has for several centuries
been the playground where anyone with a new theory can feel
free to run about a bit. So Hamlet is, or isn't, mad: is, or isn't,
Oedipal; is, or isn't, fat, a Catholic, a murderer, a saint, a
melancholic, a sceptic, a Modern, an Ancient, too young, too
old, a Calvinist, a theatre director (good or bad), a poet
(ditto), and so on. Oscar Wilde got it right in the title of his
projected essay 'Are the Commentators on Hamlet Really
Mad or only Pretending To Be?' Yet the puzzle of *Hamlet*
involves moving pieces in and out of the light until a convincing
shape appears: too much information seems to be given. The
puzzle that is *The Tempest* is of a quite different order.

Put too succinctly, the play has silences and a haunting
symmetry. Both are felt to be an invitation to interpret.
Patterns emerge easily: structures linking Caliban and Ferdinand, Caliban and Miranda, Caliban and Antonio, Prospero
and Sycorax, Antonio-with-Sebastian linked with Stephano-
with-Trinculo, and so on. Some of these will be considered
presently. For the moment, let us accept Kermode's phrase
'an exquisitely complex structure', and consider silences.

The strongly present supernatural, the controlled magic
and the sense of wonder match a curious, and unique,
bafflement in the reader. There often, undeniably, feels to be
far more going on than we are told. Adequate cause is not
always shown for the – always strong – feelings in Prospero:
he soliloquises, true; but rather than revealing to us interior
processes of thought, like Hamlet, or Macbeth, or even Leontes
in *The Winter's Tale*, Prospero makes pictures (see the great
'Ye elves of hills, brooks, standing lakes, and groves' speech
[v.i.33–57 continued in 58–82 to some extent]). Prospero
controls the action: but what the action is can puzzle everyone
in the theatre – audience, actors, and characters in the play
alike. Examining why Prospero does what he does reveals an
enigma. That, however, does not too much distress our
susceptibilities, because it matches the strange way that a
good deal of the play is unknowable.

In the long second scene, Prospero seems over-impatient
with Miranda, demanding that she understand. However
determined we as readers or spectators may be to understand
the play, many details seem to defy understanding. As A. D.
Nuttall puts it,

in the unpredictable island of *The Tempest*, we are denied that prosaic awakening which vividly refutes the night. It seems as if the poet is bent on drawing from us a different sort of credence from that ordinarily given to plays – perhaps a more primitive sort. At III.iii.83 the Shapes (we are given no clearer stage direction) carry out the banquet 'with mops and mows', and we never learn what they are or what their dance is about. At v.i.231 we are told how the sleeping sailors awoke to hear strange and horrific sounds and we are never told what made them.   (Nuttall 1967, p. 139)

Unity of time is customarily achieved by creating in the few hours of the drama a sense of the consummation of great events over a telling curve of time: but the past does not seem to dominate *The Tempest* coherently: we are given little bits of information, for example about Claribel, from whose wedding the court was sailing, or about the earlier history of the island, or about Caliban's mother: but these morsels point to a bigger hunger for information. Claribel married a Muslim, a matter of horror to a Jacobean audience: why had Alonso agreed? What was the 'one thing' Sycorax did which reduced her punishment? What were the 'grand hests' that Ariel refused? These glimpses can be suggestive, but they do not put enough pressure on the intense present.

There are, furthermore, silences of a more flinty significance. Why is Miranda's mother, Prospero's wife, so remarkably absent, so that Miranda can remember ladies-in-waiting but not her? Why, in spite of all that Prospero has told her about Alonso, does Miranda say nothing at all about him when she knows he is the father of her lover Ferdinand, and greet the courtiers as if nothing had ever gone amiss? How does Prospero travel from his state of mind towards Ferdinand at the start of Act Three, when he has him bearing logs, to his eager betrothal of him to his daughter in Act Four? Exactly how does the conspiracy of Caliban and the others cause the break-up of the masque? What does it mean that Antonio is virtually silent in the last scene? What, precisely, is the state of mind of Prospero at the end of the play? What the play doesn't say can make an unusually long list. There are so-called 'loose ends' all over the plays of Shakespeare: here we are dealing with something different.

Consider, further, the unusual poetic resonances. Like many of Shakespeare's plays, *The Tempest* is almost wholly a poem.

It has a new kind of poetry, however, new even for Shakespeare, as if in his maturity he were reaching out to make marvellously advanced experiments. Often a very great artist in his last works can be seen to be taking extraordinary risks (Beethoven springs to mind). It is true of Shakespeare. As well as experimenting with form and structure, he ventures afresh into the relations of art and illusion, nature and nurture, reason and magic, virtue and vileness: and the verbal vehicle for a great deal of new matter is first of all an extraordinary compression, as if only a small amount of what had to be said could be put into words. With the apparently absolute freedom that thought can have here, working through the beat of the five-stress lines, itself especially geared to the expression of powerful feelings, such late-Shakespearean cutting-back to linguistic spareness, with remarkable lyric effects, is in this play carried far beyond expectation.

> . . . at pick'd leisure
> Which shall be shortly single, I'll resolve you,
> Which to you shall seem probable, of every
> These happen'd accidents. . .
>
> [v.i.247–50]

Yet this is worked, kneaded in as we might put it, with a strange multivalency. The expected reverberations set up by the lines seem to have fewer limits, or no limits at all: they go in all directions.

> Be not afeard. The isle is full of noises,
> Sounds, and sweet airs, that give delight, and hurt not.
> Sometimes a thousand twangling instruments
> Will hum about mine ears; and sometimes voices,
> That, if I then had wak'd after long sleep,
> Will make me sleep again; and then, in dreaming,
> The clouds methought would open and show riches,
> Ready to drop upon me, that, when I wak'd,
> I cried to dream again.
>
> [III.ii.130–8]

These famous and magnificent lines, using subtle and sophisticated effects characteristic of the very top of the poetic skills of the English Renaissance, are spoken by no noble courtier. They are the words of the 'debosh'd [debauched] fish' Caliban. They come at the end of a low scene of silly drunken foolery, when Ariel's music of invisible tabor and drum causes a moment of terror. The scene begins in prose. It is the 'monster' Caliban who moves it into verse, half-way through, using sophisticated words like 'nonpareil' and 'jocund' on his way to that marvellous paragraph of rich sounds and dreams. His low comic on-stage auditors do not grasp what he has said – only that they'll get music for nothing.

The words reach out far beyond their being an announcement by Caliban, and go on reverberating in the silence around them. Something else, it seems, is invisibly happening. Ariel's tabor and drum were invisible: what 'reality' they might have had is a disturbing question. As A. D. Nuttall puts it:

> Playgoers are fairly well accustomed to that sane and purposive magic which saves a drowning man or refreshes him with sleep, but the music in the air, the voice crying in the wave, the 'strange, hollow and confused noise' which accompanies the vanishing of the reapers and nymphs at the end of the masque, the somnolence of Miranda – these gratuitous paranorma are more disturbing ... Ariel vanishes in thunder, the 'Shapes' carry out the table, and Alonso tells how he heard the name 'Prosper' in the withdrawing roar of the waves, and then in the wind and thunder. Again, the empirical character is strong. Experience will supply many such false configurations which have left us momentarily in doubt whether to form a natural or a supernatural interpretation. (Nuttall 1967, pp. 139, 145)

The multivalency of a few simple sounds can be kaleidoscopic, to mix the metaphor. There is, for example, more music in *The Tempest* than in any other play of Shakespeare; and some of the words to the music which 'crept by' Ferdinand 'upon the waters' (whatever that means) have a lyrical singularity which makes them among the most haunting in the language:

> Full fathom five thy father lies
> Of his bones are coral made;
> Those are pearls that were his eyes;
> Nothing of him that doth fade
> But doth suffer a sea-change
> Into something rich and strange. . .
> [I.ii.396–401]

These words both are themselves, and refer to, illusions; transformations through art itself. *The Tempest* is full of new compound words, some beginning with 'sea-' (sea-sorrow, sea-storm, sea-swallowed, sea-marge) as if even the way language works can in this play be as shifting and powerful (and in Ariel's hands as transforming) as the sea. Throughout the play, the sense of always-altering perceptions is like that which comes in sleep and with dreams: there are several wakings from sleep in the play, and six strong references to dreams. There is the same evanescence, too. Imaginative insight, which can have such power, has to be seized in the moment, however it comes:

> The cloud-capp'd towers, the gorgeous palaces,
> The solemn temples, the great globe itself,
> Yea, all which it inherit, shall dissolve,
> And, like this insubstantial pageant faded,
> Leave not a rack behind.
>
> [IV.i.152–6]

All this is only a part of that strong feeling the play can communicate that it is 'about' something just out of sight. If only whatever it is could be grasped, then essential truths about life, the universe and everything might become life-changingly clear. That silent burden of possibility in so much of the poetry is only a fraction, indeed, of the organisation of the play. It is therefore not at all surprising that a good deal of criticism has been aimed at 'explaining' this play. Because it is not so commonly seen in performance (a process which does anchor notions to some kind of reality) it is also not surprising that such 'keys' to the play are usually at best contradictory and at worst dotty.

Allegory

Romantic criticism of, and absorption of, *The Tempest*, found Prospero the wizard-like Poet, his magic that of the Romantic poet's imagination. The most insistent allegorical readings of the play, from quite early in the nineteenth century, simply extend that to the equation Prospero = Shakespeare. The location of the play in Folio does give it a certain prominence: from that fact it is easy to conclude that it was especially important to Shakespeare, and then go on to declare that that was because it was the epitome of his career. Thomas Campbell in 1838 was probably the first to make the connection: he found 'a sacredness as the last work of a mighty workman'. This notion has survived lustily, and is – especially since the establishment of the chronology appeared to make the play Shakespeare's last – still one of the first comments made by people who have heard something of *The Tempest*, that it is Shakespeare's farewell-to-his-art. The equation is indeed attractive. Prospero is so conveniently Shakespeare, consummating his career, making his final theatrical illusion, breaking his staff, drowning his book, sailing away from London to Stratford (a difficult voyage, that) and retirement. But like the late-twentieth-century invention of a homosexual Shakespeare, the lover of the Earl of Southampton, it is in fact pure invention. Just as there is not one scrap of evidence that Shakespeare ever even met Southampton (and to try to bring supporting evidence from the Sonnets is to show ignorance of the conventions of Elizabethan sonnet sequences), so there is no evidence whatever for Prospero as Shakespeare. Both seem to be necessary inventions, needed by a public that is mystified by, and therefore a little frightened of, high art, and so reassured by a devaluing equation between the work and the man. And both inventions are a crude form of allegorical reading of the works.

The great allegories of European literature – *The Divine Comedy*, *Piers Plowman*, *The Romance of the Rose*, *The Faerie Queene*, *The Pilgrim's Progress* – deliberately invite the activity of suggesting parallel meaning. The plays of Shakespeare's time, including *The Tempest*, do not. Nor were they taken as allegories when they were first written (which is when the supposed allegorical meaning would be, supposedly, strongest) as the evidence produced by Richard Levin makes so clear (Levin 1979) – though allegory was alive and active as a form at the time. Spenser's Una and Duessa in Book One of *The Faerie Queene* are named to call up sets of equivalences. Further, if Christian's burden, or roll, or river-crossing, in *The Pilgrim's*

Progress, do not stand for great spiritual experiences, then the book is in fact pretty small beer.

The start of the allegorical approaches to *The Tempest* can be dated exactly – August Wilhelm von Schlegel's lecture on the comedies of Shakespeare in Vienna in 1808. Schlegel was already a celebrated translator of Shakespeare, and the German version known as 'Schlegel-Tieck' established Shakespeare as almost the German national poet. Like Coleridge, Schlegel interpreted the genius of Shakespeare afresh. He challenged the eighteenth-century Shakespeare of 'a wild irregular genius, in whom great faults are compensated by great beauties' and presented instead a great poet, a great dramatist and a great creator of characters, with comprehensive, and indeed universal, sympathies. Shakespeare was more: 'in strength a demi-god, in profundity of view a prophet, in all-seeing wisdom a protecting spirit of a higher order'. It was Schlegel who first related Ariel to the airy elements and Caliban to the earthy, suggesting an allegory which coincides with Elizabethan and Jacobean humour-psychology.

Keats expressed the spirit of those (Romantic) times in his letter begun 14 February 1819:

> A Man's life of any worth is a continual allegory – and very few eyes can see the Mystery of his life – a life like the scriptures, figurative – which such people can no more make out than they can the hebrew Bible. Lord Byron cuts a figure – but he is not figurative – Shakespeare led a life of Allegory: his works are the comments on it.   (Forman 1947, p. 305)

After Schlegel, early interest was in Miranda, 'Eve of an enchanted Paradise'; for Heine in 1838, her prototype was 'hidden behind the stars too far off to reach my sight'. De Quincey and Thomas Campbell in England, and Montégut in France, developed the idea of relation to some parallel world outside the play. Thomas Campbell, as A. D. Nuttall writes, 'was, as far as I know, the first to make an allegorical connexion between Prospero and Shakespeare himself. Prospero drowns his book and Shakespeare takes his leave of the London theatre' (Nuttall 1967, p. 5). Montégut took this startlingly further:

Et l'histoire de l'île enchantée telle que Prospero l'expose dans ses conversations du premier acte avec Miranda, Ariel et Caliban, est-ce qu'elle ne raconte pas trait pour trait l'histoire de théâtre anglais et de la transformation que Shakespeare lui fit subir?   (quoted Nuttall, p. 5)
(*And the story of the enchanted isle as Prospero reveals it in his dialogues with Miranda, Ariel and Caliban in the first Act, is it not an account, feature by feature, of the English theatre and the transformation to which Shakespeare subjected it?*)

He goes on to identify the foul witch Sycorax with the foul English theatre of earlier times. It is illuminating to quote here Nuttall's further examples of such historical allegorising:

A similar impulse for elaboration carries Dowden as far as suggesting that Ferdinand is 'the young Fletcher in conjunction with whom Shakespeare worked upon *The Two Noble Kinsmen* and *Henry VIII*'. The twentieth century has, of course, seen hypotheses equally bizarre, if not more so. In 1925 the curious genius Robert Graves was willing to identify the drunken sailors of the play with 'Chapman and Jonson with a suggestion of Marston'. A Miss Winstanley who corresponded with Graves found in Sycorax the reputed witch Catherine de Medici and in Caliban Jesuitism and Ravaillac, who was entrusted with the task of murdering Henry IV, and is described in pamphlets as a spotted monster and a degenerate. He was, it seems, first racked and then pinched to death with red-hot pincers for the murder.   (Nuttall p. 6)

The greatest excesses have always come from the transcendentalisers, to coin a horrible word. Nuttall notes Victor Hugo, Alfred Mézières, Ruskin – even, in Daniel Wilson's *Caliban: The Missing Link* (1873) a Darwinian, evolutionary *Tempest*. Edward R. Russell in 1876 went the whole hog: Prospero is God. As Nuttall observes, 'even the reader who was prepared to find a sort of sanctity in the play as a whole has some difficulty in bowing down and worshipping the irascible old Duke of Milan as the God of his fathers' (p. 9). The most influential, however, of the nineteenth-century transcendental-allegorisers has been the American, James Russell Lowell, in *Among My Books* (1870), where 'Caliban = brute understanding, Ariel = fancy, Prospero = imagination, etc' (Kermode 1964, p. lxxxi): and Edward Dowden's far-reaching *Shakespere – A Critical Study of his Mind and Art* (London, 1875). Dowden, indeed, in a passage not mentioned by Nuttall, writes, in his chapter 'Shakespere's Last Plays':

It is not chiefly because Prospero is a great enchanter, now about to break his magic staff, to drown his book deeper than ever plummet sounded, to dismiss his airy spirits, and to return to the practical service of his Dukedom, that we identify Prospero in some measure with Shakespeare himself. It is rather because the temper of Prospero, the grave harmony of his character, his self-mastery, his calm validity of will, his sensitiveness to wrong, his unfaltering justice, and with these, a certain abandonment, a remoteness from the common joys and sorrows of the world, are characteristic of Shakespeare as discovered to us in all his latest plays. Prospero is a harmonious and fully-developed *will*. In the earlier play of fairy enchantments, *A Midsummer Night's Dream*, the 'human mortals' wander to and fro in a maze of error, misled by the mischievous frolic of Puck, the jester and clown of Fairyland. But here the spirits of the elements, and Caliban the gross genius of brute-matter, – needful for the service of life – are brought under subjection to the human will of Prospero.   (Dowden 1875, pp. 417–18).

Nuttall sums up well:

With varying degrees of seriousness and vividness, the romantic men of letters felt that when they were talking about *The Tempest* they were talking about the structure of the universe also. They felt, by and large, that *The Tempest* itself impelled them to this course, but they did not feel that they were expounding the curious feelings of a man long dead. The metaphysics they proposed was, they felt, quite as much their own as it was Shakespeare's. Ontological assertions are woven into the very fabric of their criticism.   (p. 13)

Though E. B. Wagner in 1935 proposed that *The Tempest* was an allegory of the history of the Church, the major twentieth-century allegorisers are on the whole greater transcendentalists still. E. M. W. Tillyard (1938) and G. Wilson Knight (1948) held that there was a pattern in the tragedies, which they saw as breakdown and death, symbolised by storm, with the suggestion of final reconciliation beyond the grave. This, they said, followed through to the pattern of the Romances, which all consummate in a restoration, regeneration, even resurrection. Such ideas later crystallised into altogether firmer Christianising, as we shall see.

But I pause here to mention by far the most elaborate, and in some ways the most impenetrable, of twentieth-century allegorisings, the two books by Colin Still. His first, *Shakespeare's Mystery Play, a Study of 'The Tempest'* (1921) made a second appearance, in 'an enlarged and clarified restatement' as the second part of a longer work altogether, *The Timeless Theme* of 1936. He wrote there by the help of direct textual evidence I shall show that THE TEMPEST is an imaginative mystery which is true to the spiritual experience of all mankind; that it is, in effect, a particular version of the universal theme; and that it shares not only the inner significance, but inevitably also to some extent the outward form, of every other version of the same theme. (1936, p. 134)

The centre of his method is a developed parallel between the action of *The Tempest* and, surprisingly, the initiation ceremonies of the Eleusinian adepts: he is in fact quite hard to pin down about why this should be. (The 'mystery' in his first title has to do with Gnostic mysteries, and not a play presented by a late-medieval guild, as 'Mystery Play' would normally be understood.) The Gnostic mystery cults, and Christian doctrine, spontaneous reflections of the unchanging facts of mankind's spiritual pilgrimage, gave him his analogies, and all were, he found, fused in the play, which becomes 'a dramatic representation of the Mystery of Redemption, conceived as a psychological experience and expressed in mythological form'. The whole is worked through with relentless detail, with Lesser and Greater Initiations, the Ceremony of Water, temptations offered and removed like Christ's in Milton's *Paradise Regained*; Stephano and Trinculo represent the Fall, Ferdinand ascends to the Celestial Paradise, and Prospero is both Priest and God.

Though Still asserts that only a critic who is truly a mystic can understand the mystic truths in great works of art, he has received some solemn attention: Frank Kermode called his interpretation 'improbable' (p. lxxxiii), and that is possibly over-kind.

When I was an undergraduate, I attended a dinner party at which Nevill Coghill was also a guest. He was a good Shakespeare scholar, and director, and an inspiring teacher; he spoke then about *The Tempest*, and the challenge of putting it on the stage. A mast and spar, he said, would suggest a ship instantly, and would dominate the first scene – and there, he said, you had it, making the shape with his arms: the Christian cross, a controlling image for the whole play. The waters round the island were the waters of baptism – did not the clothes come out of the water *better*? Thus the island was the kingdom of God. This was heady stuff in the Oxford of the time, and far more graspable than Colin Still's Eleusinian mysteries. It did seem to make Prospero into a sort of Christ, which raised problems, however. I don't believe that Coghill's dinner-table disquisition ever reached print. More recent Christianisers are more eager to proselytise. A strain of pious American criticism of Shakespeare has for two decades seen that curiosity 'a Christ-figure' everywhere. It appears, often, regardless of either Tudor and Stuart ways of thinking, or indeed, sometimes, of respect for textual fact. Such a chimera has, for example, been attached to 'the old fantastical duke of dark corners', Vincentio in *Measure for Measure*. A peppering of religious phrases in this play has set these critics busily fixing stained-glass images into the windows of a quite illusory chapel. It is not even as if the play's title is Christian: it echoes a phrase from Matthew 7 which itself echoes an Old Testament idea, which can mean just retribution, or moderation as a virtue, or both. 'Christ-figures' have been seen in the most wildly inappropriate characters, as Richard Levin (1979) demonstrates, including Falstaff himself. Such allegorising is not confined to Protestants. The Jesuit Peter Milward has recently given us King Lear as a Virgin Mary figure, which shows the bog-land into which allegorising can sink. In his earlier, and wayward *Shakespeare's Religious Background*, Milward tries to demonstrate that Miranda, too, is a representation of the Virgin Mary. This claim depends on acceptance of the likelihood of Shakespeare's reverence for the Virgin Mary extending so far as to include a knowledge of rather obscure French plays on the miracles of the Virgin – a Shakespeare who, we may remember, lived in a self-consciously Protestant country, was baptised, brought up, married and buried a Protestant, and saw his children baptised, brought up, and – in the only case – married, as Protestants. Moreover, Milward's Miranda-as-Virgin-Mary claim is based on Prospero's 'You have not sought her help, of whose soft grace/For the like loss I have her sovereign aid' [v.i.142–3]. These lines, Milward says, refer to the Virgin: they do not. They do not even refer to Miranda, but to Patience. The bog is deeper than such commentators imagine.

Colin Still seems much less wild by comparison. Though he has never been taken wholly seriously, allegorising is a pertinacious form, and very recently a critic has suggested that there is more life in Still's work than many have suggested.

Michael Srigley has been able to suggest his own reading of the play as an allegory of regeneration. He convincingly demonstrates that there are veins of alchemic, Paracelsian and baptismal imagery in the play, and attempts to support Still, that *The Tempest* is indeed influenced by the rituals of the Eleusinian mysteries. Perhaps the verdict has to be, again, not proven, particularly in view of the absence of contemporary support for reading drama in this way: but Srigley does open a new seam, in suggesting the possibility of the influence of the Renaissance interpretation of the *Aeneid* as an allegory of the Platonic search for truth. If Srigley is, as he seems to be, reading his allegory through Renaissance spectacles, then he and his subject warrant serious attention (Srigley 1985).

What has to be called the 'Shakespeare – the Final Phase' school of criticism, exemplified most in Dowden (and later, Furnivall) grew out of that identifying of Shakespeare with one of his characters, Prospero. So, like a character in one of his plays – though not, interestingly enough, very much like Prospero – Shakespeare had to be seen to develop from early stumblings to final maturity and serene acceptance. Thus Morton Luce in 1902, in the first Arden edition of the play, found that the structure of the Romances showed, if not carelessness, then a lack of 'concentrated artistic determination and purpose': the playwright finds the writing of plays now 'more of a recreation', though the tone is high. 'He is now approaching his fiftieth year; and his experience, if it left him sadder when he wrote his great tragedies, has now left him wiser also'. Walter Raleigh, in his *Shakespeare* (1907), in the chapter on 'The Last Phase', found a similar benevolence.

This was all too much for Lytton Strachey in 1904, who in a famous and much-reprinted essay wrote that the happy endings of the plays showed, not Shakespeare's tranquillity, but that he knew how to end a fairy-tale – and 'in this land of faery, is it right to neglect the goblins?' Shakespeare's powers had deteriorated. The reader is often bored. So was Shakespeare.

It is difficult to resist the conclusion that he was getting bored himself. Bored with people, bored with real life, bored with drama, bored, in fact, with everything except poetry and poetical dreams . . . on the one side inspired by soaring fancy to the singing of ethereal songs, and on

the other, urged by a general disgust to burst occasionally through his
torpor into bitter and violent speech.   (Strachey 1922, p. 60)

Strachey does give weight to one quality: 'The Enchanted
Island . . . has been cut adrift for ever from common sense,
and floats, buoyed up by a sea, not of waters, but of poetry'
(p. 61).

The essay was deemed offensive; but it worked. As Philip
Edwards wrote, 'The vision of the mellowed and matured
Shakespeare, sitting by the banks of the Avon, the wind
playing gently with his white hair, submerged to reappear
only furtively' (Edwards 1958, p. 3). The older allegorisers
were put more firmly in their place in an influential essay in
1927 by E. E. Stoll, a powerful senior American critic who
was among the most trenchant of that useful school of critics
who aimed at a less tuppence-coloured view of Shakespeare:
Stoll's penny-plain-ness lay in seeing Shakespeare in relation
to his contemporaries and his theatre. Thus he argued that
Ariel and Caliban did not in fact need to symbolise anything
at all. What they were, as theatrical parts, would be recognis-
able to Shakespeare's audience, and wholly explicable. To
make them symbols is in fact to diminish them: a play's
effect is reduced when characters become labels attached to
'meanings' (Stoll 1927).

The allegorisers proceeded by enclosing the play in a
sort of woolly jacket. Like some more recent iconographers,
allegorising critics used their lofty erudition with an apparently
determined vagueness about mere detail in the plays. The
same could be said of some myth-and-ritualisers.

Myth and ritual

Asked, we are told, to fill some blank pages at the end of *The
Waste Land*, T. S. Eliot somewhat capriciously added Notes.
The same stimulus that drove many readers of those Notes,
just after the First World War, to Jessie L. Weston's *From
Ritual to Romance* and Sir James Frazer's *The Golden Bough* to
look for exciting clues to a seductively 'significant' poem sent
the new readers of anthropology and comparative religion into
schematising Shakespeare. The last plays shone with promise.

That is not so very extraordinary: romance is always close to myth. The very invitation which *The Tempest* extends seemed to be addressed to those critics who could write about the great and apparently universal symbols of Royal Death and Rebirth, of Vegetation Rites, of Fertility, and the rest. The key word was 'universal'. The argument went like this: great art is a process, a movement of events which relate to the greatest experiences of human nature. If you look at great works of art in the right way, you can see that they all contain the same elements. If you look at the great myths of mankind, from anywhere in the world, the right way, you find exactly the same elements. In both, art and myth, they appear not as *dramatis personae*, or particular shaped sequences, but as symbols of something altogether larger and more universal. The critical approach is close to that of imposing allegorical meaning on to a play or poem or novel, with the difference that now the imposed meaning is something altogether more awesome, and even grander than the fantasies of the Christian-isers. For whereas they find mere 'Christ-figures' everywhere, here in this exalted air even Christ's crucifixion is itself only a symbol of something infinitely deep in universal human experience – the sacrifice of the young prince for the salvation of the tribe. That this need for assertion of a universal humanity, with emphasis on the infinitely significant value of sacrifice, came after the First World War, is not surprising. Frazer in particular seemed to be drawing aside a veil to show, deeply reassuringly, something of what C. G. Jung later called the 'collective unconscious'.

Drama, moreover, contains another element which seems to make it perfect for such equations. It enacts for a community a performance with a beginning, a middle and an end – indeed, it can easily be said to be doing this on behalf of the community. That very progression, that longer and more complex development from beginning to end, is an ingredient not always found in myths, which are usually fairly uncomplica-ted in plot. Drama is performed by special people, and there is some stress on them being the right people, properly capable of it. So drama clearly has a powerful ritual function: and as such is part of a stream of human experience that goes back to the dawn of time, as the phrases have it. The priests of that ancient time, the correct performers, have merely changed their appearance slightly to become holders of Equity cards.

So here was apparently another way into studying the universals of humanity, by studying rituals. (That this under-standing of 'rituals' was so severely limited as to be virtually useless was not apparent at the time. Frazer worked entirely from written accounts: and did not consider his own position, either ideologically or methodologically – he did not consider his own daily routine as 'ritual', for example.) At the time, humanity's great religions, and the supposedly even older folk-customs and rituals, seemed to provide stunning material with which to open up not just a new window into some plays of Shakespeare, but comprehensive understanding of the whole work.

Though early in the twentieth century it had been noticed how Shakespeare at the end seemed preoccupied with the theme of reconciliation, and the importance of the royal children and their survival, creating a new world out of what their parents had nearly destroyed, the classic statement of the appeal to myth came a third of the way through the century, in G. Wilson Knight's enormously influential short essay 'Myth and Miracle', published in 1929. Here the words 'myth' and 'universal' are constantly applied to the four last plays, and particularly *The Tempest*. In the same volume, *The Crown of Life*, which opens with 'Myth and Miracle', is a long chapter, 'The Shakespearian Superman: an Essay on *The Tempest*'. This is less startling, though it does contain one influential suggestion – that 'The poetry is pre-eminently in the events themselves, which are intrinsically poetic' (Knight 1948, p. 224). In that chapter, there is a sentence about *The Tempest* which sums up much of the first chapter's thesis: 'A myth of creation woven from his total work by the most universal of poets is likely to show correspondences with other well-authenticated results of the racial imagination' (p. 224).

To get to his much-referred-to 'universals', Knight has a good deal to do with the words 'mystic' and 'mysticism'. He argues that there is a twelve-year period which takes Shakespeare from the problem plays through the great trage-dies towards a spiritual fulfilment. Note 'spiritual': on the first page of 'Myth and Miracle' he writes, 'That spiritual quality which alone causes great work to endure through the centuries should be the primary object of our attention' (p. 9). He finds that 'tragedy is merging into mysticism, and what is left to say must be said not in terms of tragedy, but of miracle and myth' – which leads him to *Pericles* and *The Winter's Tale*. He writes of the apparition of the goddess Diana in *Pericles*, 'A reader sensitive to poetic atmosphere must necessarily feel the awakening light of some religious or metaphysical truth symbolized in the plot and attendant machinery' (p. 14). The Vision of Jupiter in *Cymbeline* has 'clear religious and universal significance' (p. 16): in view of 'the mystic significance' of it, 'we shall find it quite reasonable that he [Shakespeare] should attempt a universal statement in direct language concerning the implication of his plot' by means of it (p. 19). Knight sums up, on the three plays before *The Tempest*, 'these miraculous and joyful conquests of life's tragedy are the expression, through the medium of drama, of a state of mind or soul in the writer directly in knowledge . . . of a mystic and transcendent fact as to the true nature and purpose of the sufferings of humanity' (p. 23).

Thus 'a prophetic criticism could, if *The Tempest* had been lost, have nevertheless indicated what must be its essential nature, and might have hazarded its name' (p. 23). He opposes 'tempest-symbolism' to music, and 'the hate-theme' to love, ideas he finds consummated in *The Tempest*. The 'predominating symbols' of the four plays 'are loss in tempest and revival to the sounds of music. It is about twelve years from the inception of this lonely progress of the soul to the composition of *The Tempest*'. On the island, Prospero is 'master of his lonely magic. He has been there for twelve years' (p. 24). So '*The Tempest* is at the same time a record of Shakespeare's spiritual progress and a statement of the vision to which that progress has brought him' (p. 27). We are here, according to Knight, in a world of timeless absolutes. 'The progress from spiritual pain and despairing thought through stoic acceptance to a serene and mystic joy is a universal rhythm in the spirit of man' (p. 29). Concluding, he writes:

> As for my contention that the Final Plays of Shakespeare must be read as myths of immortality, that is only to bring his work into line with other great works of literature. Tragedy is never the last word: theophanies and reunions characterise the drama of the Greeks: they, too, tell us that 'with God all things are possible'.   (p. 30)

Sixty years on, the reader must be struck by both the assurance and the vagueness of this immensely influential piece. The uplifting tone and the woolliness about detail can, in fact, be alarming. In the passage above, he is surely wrong to assert that 'tragedy is never the last word' and to use the quotation from St Paul for a sentimental, and again wrong, thought about the Greek drama. He is set on avoiding pain altogether.

> It is, indeed, noticeable that these plays do not aim at revealing a temporal survival of death: rather at the thought that death is a delusion. What was thought dead is in reality alive. In them we watch the fine flowers of a mystic state of soul bodied into the forms of drama.   (p. 22)

There is something very wrong indeed here. Death was not a delusion for Mamillius or Antigonus in *The Winter's Tale* nor for the mothers of Caliban or, presumably, Miranda, in *The Tempest*. Nor was death a delusion for William Shakespeare; nor is it for you or me, dear reader. 'The fine flowers of a mystic state of soul' are meretricious comfort.

Yet the essay was seminal. The last plays were central to all that Knight wrote (and performed) of Shakespeare. A considerable body of his own work, and that of others like Derek Traversi, grew directly from that first essay. He wrote persuasively about themes common to two or more of the last plays, and his work had the attraction of fresh scientific observation. The binary oppositions, not only love and hate but also tempest and music, and so on, gave the sense of looking at an important, and previously hidden, structure. Moreover, he made these themes not only immediate to the whole play, giving it again a Coleridgean organic unity: but at the same time the last plays were seen again to consummate the whole Shakespearean corpus, which satisfied the popular hunger for Shakespeare the Developing Artist now that Dowden's 'On the Heights', 'In the Depths' were discredited. Just as the boiling-together of world-wide myths and rituals by Frazer had seemed to reveal new chemical elements in human experience, so Knight seemed to be able to relate Shakespeare to common life – not just in Western post-Renaissance societies, but to all humanity. And Knight's opposites, as he developed them, overlapped with the flooding of literary studies by the binary systems of anthropological and linguistic 'structuralism'.

Not everyone could do it as Wilson Knight had done it. In 1958, John Crow, listing 'Deadly Sins of Criticism, or, Seven Ways to Get Shakespeare Wrong', included Arrogance: 'Let's all hunt for Fisher Kings and Dying Gods and ignore the fact that Mr Eliot wrote *The Waste Land* after, and not before, partaking of Miss Weston's good wine' (Crow, 1958) – a telling point. (The punning allusion is to the 1927 novel by T. F. Powys, *Mr Weston's Good Wine*.) An influential offshoot from Knight was C. L. Barber's *Shakespeare's Festive Comedy* of 1959, which set out to show how close comedy could be to the spirit of ancient English festivals. Barber took Shakespeare's comedies only up to *Twelfth Night*, though he wrote a separate essay on *The Winter's Tale* (1964). He had the advantage of appearing to deal in much more specific detail than Knight, and he won a generation of converts. Yet his work also now produces unease. For example, there has been much pronouncement about Saturnalia, in relation to *Twelfth Night*, without any agreement about what that, or Misrule, or whatever, means. Over-confident assertions about life in England have to be treated with some caution when they are made out of a life-experience many thousands of miles away from England; not to mention four centuries in time – and Olivia's household is in Illyria, anyway.

A good deal of caution has gathered round the work of Northrop Frye. The most powerful disciple of Knight, Frye too, focuses his work in Shakespearean comedy by keeping the Romances firmly in view. He, too, brings in the whole corpus. He, too, likes to see systems: by means of such constructions he is able to show that comedy, not tragedy, is the proper form; 'tragedy is really implicit or uncompleted comedy', he wrote in his important 'The Argument of Comedy' . . . 'comedy contains a potential tragedy within itself' (Frye 1949, p. 65). He takes the relationship between the genres further than Knight, finding a cycle that imitates what he asserts is the natural cycle of birth, death, rebirth – the rhythm of the seasons, and the basis, he says, of humanity's enduring myths. Comedy is paramount because it points beyond death: and the New Testament becomes a primary text. 'From the point of view of Christianity, tragedy is an episode in that larger scheme of redemption and resurrection to which Dante gave the name of *commedia*' (1949, p. 66) Paradoxically, Frye is harder to pin down than Knight – paradoxically, because Frye touches harder edges than 'mysticism'. Even so, his observations have been revered. His notion of the escape to, and return from, the 'green world', has permeated widely. His manner of *ipse dixit* has been particularly admired, especially in North America.

But Frye, even more than Knight, is open to attack. The distillation of so much mythological and other material gets perilously close to being meaningless. Something is wrong with the very perspective to which Frye appeals in the title of his work to which *The Tempest* is most relevant, *A Natural Perspective: The Development of Shakespearean Comedy and Romance* (1965). It gives us the play as viewed from a very long way away. This makes, as always, for attractive writing – Frye is always readable: more so than Knight – but many plays are briefly touched, and the process is of amalgamation into a surprisingly small compass. The telescope is again held the wrong way round. The effect is momentarily interesting, but it doesn't assist navigation. His declaration that *The Tempest* rediscovers the logic of the earlier romantic comedies, moving from confusion to identity, from sterility to renewed life, is ultimately sentimental. We are, he says, lifted out of the world of ordinary experiences into a world perfected by the human imagination. To which the acute reader replies, 'Yes, but. . .' *The Tempest* is a more complex work, and its end is by a long way more problematical, than Frye suggests.

The attention given to the Romances by Knight and Frye (and Barber) was for an important reason. In these plays conventional realism seemed less demanding, and the plays could feel freer, apparently allowing the underlying myths more immediate presence. The archetypes, it could be claimed, were in their least displaced form. Knight, and others, make enormous claims. He wrote that in Shakespeare's theatre,

a common store of racial wisdom for centuries untapped is now released, as Prospero releases Ariel; and the highly responsible artist has himself to explore and exploit the wide areas of imaginative truth apparently excluded (though perhaps in some sense surveyed and transcended) by Christian dogma.   (1948, p. 227)

So much myth-and-ritual criticism is either plain wrong (death as a delusion) or makes the plays more trivial than ordinary experience of them suggests. Shakespeare's characters talking (and doing things in brackets) are so much more complex: who can decide definitively how Miranda 'should' play the second scene? The subtle richness of that problem is far and away more informative about the Human Condition than all the Universal Symbols ever asserted.

I do prefer my Shakespeare neither Knighted, Barbered nor Fryed. In this I am not alone. Having expressed disillusion with D. G. James's 1967 attempt to follow Knight, Philip Edwards, for example, is more seriously disturbed by D. Traversi's *Shakespeare: The Last Phase* (1954), where it is maintained that the symbolic movements point to the acquirement of 'maturity', identified as 'a balanced view of life'.

> The reduction of the complexity of Shakespeare to a striving towards a balanced view of life seems to me typical of the pallidness of all interpretations of the last plays which insist that they are symbolic utterances. There is an appearance (there is certainly a claim) that the depths are being opened, riches are being revealed. But it is an appearance only. It is a disservice to Shakespeare to pretend that one is adding to his profundity by discovering that his plots are symbolic vehicles for ideas and perceptions which are, for the most part, banal, trite and colourless. The 'symbols' are so much more fiercely active, potent, rich, complex as themselves than as what they are made to convey. When they are translated, they do not have a tithe of their own magnitude. . . . Sentimental religiosity, in the sense of a vague belief in a vague kind of salvation, and vague tremors at the word 'grace' – so long as it is decently disengaged from Christianity; platitudinous affirmations of belief in fertility and re-creation; and insistence on the importance of maturity and balance: these are the deposits of Shakespeare's last plays once the solvent of parabolic interpretation has been applied, but these are not what the reader or audience observes in Pericles' reunion with Marina, the Whitsun Pastorals, Leontes' denial of the oracle or the wooing of Ferdinand and Miranda. The power of suggestion, which is one of the striking features of the last plays, is positively decreased by the type of criticism we are considering.   (Edwards 1958, p. 11)

4 Structures

Imagery

Of the symbol-searchers Knight, in particular, influenced, for good, those critics who expound the imagery in Shakespeare's plays, by, as Wolfgang Clemen put it, leading us 'to regard the imagery as expressive of a certain symbolism which, in Mr Knight's view, can disclose to us the meaning of the play better than anything else' (Clemen 1951, p. 16). Caroline Spurgeon's *Shakespeare's Imagery* . . . (1935) is still an intriguing book, because of her aim, expressed in the second part of her title . . . *and What It Tells Us*. She was engaged in the quest for Shakespeare's psyche. His imagery, she felt, properly arranged and considered, would uncover his innermost being as unconsciously revealed. She was a Romantic at heart, of course, trying to get to his soul, but this time by means of his Freudian slips, whereby we reveal accidentally what we 'really' feel. Figures of speech in Shakespeare, when assembled into columns and read off another way, show consistencies that Shakespeare's genius, she assumes, was unaware of. Thus her famous generalisations about disease imagery in *Hamlet* or clothing imagery in *Macbeth* were less significant than her 'discovery' that Shakespeare didn't like dogs, especially dogs who were fed bits at table: that he hated sweet things; and so on. Her work had enthusiastic successors, some like E. A. Armstrong (1946), pursuing even more doubtful phantoms; others, like Wolfgang Clemen, using discipline. (It was Clemen, indeed, who first brought to prominence the pioneering Walter Whiter, who wrote in 1794 "*A Specimen of a Commentary on Shakespeare*. Containing I. Notes on *As You Like It*. II. An attempt to explain and illustrate various passages, on a new principle of criticism, derived from Mr Locke's doctrine of the association of ideas.") Clemen pointed out the way that in *The Tempest* the 'sea-storm' sets in motion one of the main streams of imagery: and how, also, 'except for *A Midsummer Night's Dream* and *King Lear*, there is no play of Shakespeare's in which so many plants, fruits or animals appear' but, compared to 'the nature-world of *A Midsummer Night's Dream* . . . there are fewer flowers, more weeds, roots and fruits of the country', with striking figurative effect (Clemen 1951, p. 187). He observed, too, that the courtiers use notably less imagery than Prospero, Ariel and Caliban. His conclusion, on *The Tempest*, is worth quoting in full:

Examining the distribution of imagery in the whole play we may notice that, compared to the tragedies, we find a greater number of lengthy passages which consist exclusively of images. The action which permeates the whole drama again and again concentrates and is focused into densely woven clusters of images. Several times these rich and cumulative imagery-passages occur close to the end of a scene, as if it were Shakespeare's purpose to impress upon us the setting and the peculiar atmosphere of the whole before a new part of the action is to begin. Towards the end of the play such passages as are saturated in imagery grow even more frequent, especially in the great valedictory speeches of Prospero and in the masque. When the play has ended there remains in our imagination not only the remembrance of the characters which we saw on the stage, but also – and perhaps equally enduring – the vision of that strange nature-world.

The examination of the imagery in *The Tempest* showed how vividly, sensuously and precisely this nature-world was represented. As we have already said, this concreteness and realness, conveyed through the imagery, constitutes a counterpart to the world of the supernatural in this play. The supernatural, in being based on firm reality, gains probability and convincing power.   (Clemen 1951, p. 194)

Frank Kermode notes that 'the paucity of imagery in *The Tempest* has often been remarked. It has been replaced by a more decorous control of event, which gives the event itself primary significance, and requires that verse and image shall not be such as to distract the attention from it' (1964, p. lxxx). He is, however, on a different, and altogether wider, track:

There is [in *The Tempest*] little of the kind of language which extensively examines the similitudes by which its ideas are decorated, but a great deal of the kind which simulates the language of men in a state of profound sensation, progressing from idea to idea by means of pun, or by associations more or less consciously relevant. Thus:

> having both the key
> Of officer and office, set all hearts i'the'state
> To what tune pleas'd his ear;
>
> [i.ii.83–5]

> she that from whom
> We all were sea-swallow'd, though some
> cast again,
> And by that destiny to perform an act

Whereof what's past is prologue; what
    to come
In yours and my discharge.

[ɪɪ.i.245–9]

Metaphor gleams momentarily, and is rarely extensive enough to be catalogued and analysed. In the same way the basic rhythm of the iambic pentameters becomes more ghostly, a burthen heard faintly through the flux of thought. Shakespeare is still interested in the formal figures and tropes, but, like the beat of the pentameter, they are swamped by the involutions of a language which is artificially natural, and denied the auditor's attention, which is directed to the relationship between the characters' interests and the developing situation. (Kermode 1964, pp. lxxviii–lxxix)

And Anne Barton moves the whole subject on yet again:

The situation is further complicated by the fact that *The Tempest* is charged with meaning of an essentially non-verbal kind. Wilson Knight has pointed out that the action of this play is in itself poetic, that Shakespeare could afford to strip the verse of extended, formal images precisely because the whole work is a gigantic metaphor. The plot in itself has some of the self-sufficient complexity of myth material. Certainly it is true that the play stills itself around a number of stage pictures, visual images out of which many of the fundamental qualities of the dialogue seem to grow, but which remain independent of it: the wreck, the various tableaux of the masque in Act ɪv. Ariel as a harpy, the shapes which dance about the enchanted banquet, Ferdinand bearing logs, the spirit hounds hunting Caliban and his companions, or Ferdinand and Miranda discovered at chess. More perhaps than with any other work of Shakespeare's, this is a drama which the actors could walk through silently and still manage to convey much of its essential nature. The grouping of characters, the very physical appearance of Ariel and Caliban, of Miranda, or Prospero in his magician's robes, possesses significance. Nor should one forget the omni-present background of music, the sheer number of songs in the play and the manner in which they draw to themselves and translate emotions which words alone seem inadequate to express. (Barton 1968, pp. 17–18)

Verbal design

At the same time, it is a play that seems to have been written for radio. Reuben A. Brower demonstrated the intricacy of its verbal interweaving: a complex pattern built entirely of words, a 'metaphorical design' in which the 'elements are linked through almost inexhaustible analogies' (Brower 1951, p. 95). This extraordinary echoic quality of the play had been noticed by earlier critics, notably Una Ellis-Fermor, who wrote well on the importance of the changes rung on the word 'sea' and its compounds, an example that showed how the imagery of the play is determined structurally (Ellis-Fermor 1936, p. 269). Fifteen years later, Brower found 'six main continuities . . . "strange-wondrous", "sleep-and-dream", "sea-tempest", "music-and-noise", "earth-air", "slavery-freedom", and "sovereignty-conspiracy" (Brower 1951, p. 91) [he lists seven, in fact]. These are all connected, he found, through a 'key metaphor . . . which is "sea-change" (p. 111), a process of Ovidian metamorphosis. The debate about whether *The Tempest* is, as it were, a play for radio or television will no doubt continue: it is a play which is apparently endlessly rich in its verbal and visual patterns.

Dramatic design

When the play is trodden out on the boards, different patterns emerge, a set of structural principles quite separate from the verbal and visual ones, and just as important. In 1960, David William wrote:

> *The Tempest* is not only a difficult play; it is uniquely beautiful; and its difficulty is that its beauty lies principally in the region of its interior action. The climaxes of *Othello* or *Twelfth Night*, for example, are physically demonstrable; there is explicitly significant action to establish them; but the climax of *The Tempest* is a moral decision . . . Prospero's renunciation of vengeance is the resolution of the play; everything else leads up to it, and upon it the destinies of all the characters (himself included) depend.

William shows clearly the state of high feeling in Prospero in i.ii as, after twelve years, his plans mature in a few hours. Not only is this the second shortest play:

> it has fewer scenes than any. The action is continuous and confined; in fact, the unities of time and place are observed more stringently than any formulation demands. These facts alone bespeak a deliberate restriction of subject unusual for Shakespeare. Moreover, nearly a quarter of the play is devoted to exposition. That is a very high proportion – too

high for theatrical comfort, if it is *mere* exposition. Fortunately it is not, for it is animated and sustained by continually inventive characterisation, and integrated with the establishment of the physical and moral background of the play.   (William 1971, p. 435)

One powerful dramatic pattern, we may note, has as its key, Prospero's 'The rarer action is / In virtue than in vengeance' [IV.i.26]. There is emerging here an opposition between what are properly 'poetic' structures, and 'theatrical' structures, a binary system on a different plane to what was implied in the 'radio/television' analogy I created above. Moreover, as soon as we allow planes to shift, other binary systems come into sight, strikingly alive and suggestive, held together, like double stars, in a gravitational bond – like sovereignty and conspiracy, for example. Who in the play is sovereign? Prospero? Alonso? Stephano? Caliban? Who is conspiring? Prospero? Antonio? Alonso? Caliban?

Dramatic polarities

That *The Tempest* reveals patterns has long been known – in effect, ever since the seventeenth-century offshoots and adaptations set out to fill in blanks in the symmetries. What is new in the twentieth century, and very particularly as it draws to a close, is the understanding of the ideological implications of those oppositions. To recapitulate for a moment: Geoffrey Bullough in 1975 summed up, with acknowledgements to A. H. Gilbert in 1915:

Shakespeare conceived his plot and characters in parallel or antithetical pairs. Two fathers (Prospero and Alonso) who have been enemies, have children (Miranda and Ferdinand) who fall in love. The two brothers Propsero and Antonio are opposed in nature. The island has contained two kinds of supernatural, black (with Sycorax) and white (with Prospero). The children of these two opposed magicians, (Caliban and Miranda) are entirely antithetical. The shipwrecked voyagers fall into two parties, the nobles and the clowns. There are two conspiracies, one against Alonso, the other against Prospero, with Antonio and Sebastian in the one, and Stephano and Trinculo in the other. Prospero's two servants, Ariel and Caliban, are continually contrasted with one another both in character and actions, and so on.   (Bullough 1975, p. 271)

Frank Kermode indicates extensions:

The Tempest makes much of this [virginity associated with magic power], and also of the contrast betwen the unchastity of the natural man, in whom cultivation has brought forth only 'the briers and darnell of appetites' and the man of better nature, represented under this aspect by Ferdinand; the comparison at the level of ideas is expressed in their attitudes to Miranda, and at the level of narrative in their reactions to the duty of log-bearing which Prospero enforces upon them severally; to Ferdinand it is a sanctified labour, it physics pain with delight; it is the restraint – horticulturally one might say, the cutting-back – from which the fruit of good develops: but to Caliban it is a discipline of fear.   (pp. lvii–lviii)

Caliban parallels Miranda in that he 'never saw a woman' [III.ii.98], and in the accounts of their education and their reactions to the sight of the nobleman. Prospero's anger at Caliban's ingratitude for the use of reason parallels his anger at Antonio's ingratitude for ducal power. 'Antonio and Sebastian react to their first sight of Caliban exactly as their inferiors, Stephano and Trinculo, had. They speculate on his possible market value' (Barton 1968, p. 176). D. J. Palmer, in a passage too long to quote here, illuminates the parallels and contrasts even more thoroughly. He concludes,

the complexity of Shakespeare's pattern is illustrated by Caliban. In that he cannot respond to Prospero's attempts to teach him, he is a foil to Miranda; in that he resents the tasks imposed upon him by Prospero, he is a foil to Ferdinand; in that he plots with Trinculo and Stephano, he is a foil to Antonio; in that he urges his fellow conspirators to ignore the flashy clothes left by Prospero to distract them, he is a foil to Stephano and Trinculo. He is both villain and clown – in one respect an unnatural hybrid monster, in another sense the savage man of pastoral tradition; and he might even be claimed as the only American in Shakespeare. The whole is greater than the sum of its parts.

(Palmer 1968, pp. 15–16)

Such symmetrical pairings are an extension from Shakespeare's more usual arrangement of scenes, which we recognise here too. Thus II.ii, which begins with the monster Caliban carrying logs for his master, contrasts with the beginning of the next scene, III.i, where the prince, Ferdinand, carries logs for his mistress. The exquisiteness of *The Tempest* lies partly in this network of correspondences – which is itself only half the story, as the very network itself corresponds to, or opposes, unique silences and opacities.

Polarities in the sources

Both a system of correspondences, and that open-ness to interpretation, Shakespeare could have been aware of in his presumed sources for the play – 'presumed', because, like *A Midsummer Night's Dream* only more so, *The Tempest* has no obvious source. We should be blind not to see Florio's Montaigne, the *Aeneid*, Golding's Ovid, a Jonson masque or two, as contributing ideas and even passages: but in the sense that *As You Like It* is Lodge's *Rosalynde*, or *The Winter's Tale* is built out of Greene's *Pandosto*, there is nothing. Apart, of course, from what are called the Bermuda Pamphlets, giving accounts of the disappearance at sea of Sir Thomas Gates, on his way in 1609 to be Acting-Governor of the new colony of James Town until Lord de la Warr could take over, and his party's survival, extrication and arrival in Virginia. Geoffrey Bullough (1975, pp. 238–41) gives a lucid account, and prints extracts, as do the Arden and Oxford editions of the play. And even in Bullough's scholarly descriptions, the sense of double standards comes over strongly. The official statements visible in the pamphlets maintain that government policy on colonisation was firmly on course – lest the City should panic and subscriptions to the venture should not continue. Also clearly visible, however, is the admission of calamitous 'dissension and ambition' among the leaders in the Virginia colony, and 'the idleness and bestial sloth of the common sort' – though it is suggested that these were scandalous reports spread by 'unruly youth' recently returned from America. Moreover, the accounts of the shipwreck of the *Sea-Venture* show it as both hideously dreadful and at the same time miraculous – both a calamity and evidence of Providence at work. The storm, it seems, was both elemental and moral.

Geoffrey Bullough writes (perhaps, we may feel, a little over-confidently):

> The playwright in search of a plot found in the Virginian pamphlets promising features, including a tempest; shipwreck; a haunted island of ill repute but beautiful and fertile, though uninhabited and almost inaccessible; a mingling of social classes – nobles, gentlemen, tradesmen, labourers, mariners, natives well- and ill-disposed – dissensions leading to dangerous divisions and conspiracies.

The way Bullough continues is significant:

At least as important for Shakespeare were the ethical ideas and lessons embodied in the pamphlets, such as the need (especially in perilous situations) of firm leadership and a strong governor. . . . The importance of hard work and self-control were also shown, for the Virginian colony was almost destroyed by idleness, ignorance, greed, and lust.   (Bullough 1975, p. 242)

Earlier, Bullough has remarked;

The Tempest is not a play about colonisation, but when James I and his courtiers saw it performed at Whitehall while the controversy about the settlement was still hot, they must have seen – and been intended to see – many subtle allusions to it.   (pp. 241–2)

To what it was that these subtle allusions were made, Bullough goes on to explain.

To justify colonisation in the name of religion and civilisation was one aim of several works written on behalf of the adventurers to America. To preach the Gospel to every nation was incumbent upon good Christians; to educate the educable was a humane task; to domesticate the wilderness, to win profit by trade and manufactures, to extend the royal realms by taking possession of empty or ill-used lands, were all praise-worthy activities. . . . Recalcitrant or treacherous natives, it was generally agreed, should be ruled firmly, even harshly, for Sir Thomas Gates found 'how little a fair and noble intreatie workes upon a barbarous disposition'.

All these ideas [Bullough continues] came into Shakespeare's mind and affected the characterisation and texture of his play. He was not writing a didactic work; nevertheless approval of the Virginia Company's aims, and recognition of its difficulties seem to be implied in his depiction of Prospero, Caliban, and the intruders into the island. Prospero is the good, authoritarian Governor; more, he is like the Providence which in the Bermudan ship-wreck brought the ship near to the shore that its people might escape, and gave them the means to life and to escape from their predicament. Hence was derived the conception of Prospero as an all-wise controller of events, plaguing sinners for their own good, and both testing and advising Ferdinand.   (pp. 244–5)

Now, all this is very tidy, to put it no higher – a Shakespeare approving of the Virginia Company's aims, which include treating natives harshly, and playing Providence to plague sinners for their own good: it is, ultimately, a nationalist position, to be expected of the National Poet. J. P. Brockbank, however, seems to be reading different sources as well as a different play, though they are the same Bermuda Pamphlets and Shakespeare's *The Tempest*. Instead of a moral about the Governor's role with expansionary market forces, and company necessity, and the approval of harsh (but deserved, of course) treatment of natives, Brockbank finds that,

> the pieties of the prose accounts are more than conventional; they owe their awed intensity to the sequences of catastrophe and miracle that the voyages endured. We need not hesitate to treat the play as allegory since that is how Shakespeare's contemporaries treated the actual event. After God had delivered the seamen from the 'most dreadful Tempest' of 'tumultuous and malignant' winds, the authority of the Governor is required to deliver them from what *The True Declaration* calls 'the tempest of Dissention'.   (Brockbank 1966, p. 385)

In other words, the prime part of the Governor's role is to let himself be used by God to deliver the English company from two tempests, one elemental and one social. As far as Prospero is Governor at all, this is closer to the climax of Shakespeare's play, Prospero's moral decision to show to 'the three men of sin' virtue not vengeance. Bullough's position (and his is only the most recent of many expressions of it – for documentation see Frey 1979) is too unsympathetic to a whole compass-card of polarities, those interior structural pairings so characteristic of *The Tempest*. Thus Prospero at that moral climax can be thought of as the victim dealing with his attackers, the ruler with his usurper, the good man and his evil brother, the father and his daughter's fiancé's father, and so on.

Richard Marienstras exhilaratingly explores such pairings in the 'sources', showing how the fabulous accounts of journeys, from most ancient times, made a synthesis between the real and the imaginary, truth and fantasy, the literal reality and metaphor. The fantastic seems always about to become real, and reality is on the point of becoming fantastic – 'one of the most disconcerting aspects of *The Tempest*' (Marienstras 1985, p. 161). Moreover, the voyagers found people living lives of earlier times but in the present, and 'far becomes so near that the travellers had to recreate familiar distances' (p. 163). The comforting oppositions, of civilisation and barbarity, good and evil, natural goodness and fallen nature, had to be simplified; recently discovered humans had to be right at the bottom of the hierarchy, and far away, and so made compatible with the symbolic universe of the narrator. Yet their lands held riches, and sensual temptations, and an infinite number of qualities: monsters as well. Thus 'whoever succumbed to the temptations engendered monsters' (p. 165). There was no room for plurality of cultures: monsters, marvels and riches came from nature alone. In the Bermuda Pamphlets each event is made to fall into place: and 'the uncertainties of the world of *The Tempest* are like reading a traveller's tale' (p. 172). Caliban is particularly threatening, not only 'furthest' but also 'nearest' with his passions and instinct; his anarchy, destruction, violence and danger threaten to shatter the norms that Elizabethan culture imposed. His attempted rape of Miranda was the triple transgression of a fallen creature: he attempted to satisfy his desires in defiance of the rules; he, an inferior, wanted the daughter of a Duke; and as guest he plotted to assassinate his host, Prospero. Prospero had taken him in as human. He had then made him his servant; shut him up; and finally hunted him as a wild beast, with dogs. As Caliban is both the near and the far, so Ariel is both desire and censure, and so again the conclusion of the play is both union and separation, or marriage. For, for Shakespeare,

> the Golden Age is not to be found on the Isles of the Blessed, but in the discoveries, visions and hopes of men. It is an ideal that only the human will can bring into being, on condition that men agree upon what the natural order is, make the effort to control their appetites, discipline their desires and promote harmony. That is what accounts for the overwhelming impression of sadness that the play transmits through its happy ending.   (p. 183)

Post-structuralism

It is possible to find that the compass plays tricks. Prospero and Caliban are an obvious north and south: except that, as we shall see, Caliban can become north; and indeed, the so-obvious structure can deconstruct itself altogether, so that there are no longer any binary oppositions at all, and each term inheres in the other. Further still, it can appear that this deconstruction is itself visible in the 'sources'. The Bermuda Pamphlets were the outcrop of a vivid contemporary interest, particularly urgent to the merchants and courtiers (and

Shakespeare held a court appointment) around James I – who requested this play to open his 1611–12 winter season. Like the twentieth-century critics who see Shakespeare automatically supporting the Virginia Company, the court would be eager to see a Prospero who was 'one of us', Old World, known, recognised, part of the system. The strange, the other, the monstrous is the undisciplined rabble, whether 'layabouts' (Bullough's word) in your own group who rebel instead of Furthering the Enterprise, or totally unregenerable natives who don't even make good servants, and like Caliban, or the Australian Aborigines, or the South African Bushmen, have to be turned into beasts and hunted down. There are Chinese boxes here. In what follows, we shall have to hold in mind the development of arguments to reverse the polarities of Prospero and Caliban, and then to deconstruct the very paired opposites themselves, because they are themselves the products of loaded assumptions, both in James's court (and thus in the pamphlets) and in twentieth-century critics' minds. To anticipate; Prospero can be seen as a sitting target. So can Bullough. But the new riflemen themselves, the deconstructing critics, are only slightly less open to be shot at.

The New World

Shakespeare set his play on an island in the Mediterranean, somewhere between Africa and Italy. It is worth pausing for a moment to ask whether *The Tempest* is a New World play at all. E. E. Stoll, making hay in 1927 with enthusiasts for Shakespeare-promoting-America, noted some writers'

> great pains to endeavour to prove acquaintance on Shakespeare's part with the promoters of colonising in Virginia, and sympathy with their motives and aspirations. . . . Shakespeare himself says not a word to that effect. Spenser, Daniel, Drayton and the rest sing of the New World and Virginia, but not Shakespeare. . . . There is not a word in *The Tempest* about America or Virginia, colonies or colonising, Indians or tomahawks, maize, mocking-birds or tobacco. Nothing but the Bermudas, once barely mentioned as a far-away place, like Tokio or Mandalay. His interest and sympathy Shakespeare keeps to himself. (Stoll 1927, p. 487).

Stoll, who enjoyed skirmishing, wanted to put the interest

back on Shakespeare's play, not the highways and byways of the foundation of the American nation. Some recent critics' passionate elevation of Caliban as a victim of the Old World's colonisation of the New may be motivated by something other than an essential point about Shakespeare's play. Some modern American attacks, for example, on vicious British colonising policy, at the time of *The Tempest* and after, must surely, in the late twentieth century, be a projection of some dismay about the foreign policy of America itself since the Second World War – the passion of the attack on British policy is too shrill.

Those who argue that he did not need to know the Bermuda Pamphlets to write *The Tempest* have a certain suggestiveness on their side, but little more. Certainly there were shipwrecks and islands a-plenty from Homer, the *Aeneid* and the Acts of the Apostles, onward. Erasmus's *Naufragium*, for example, translated in 1606, is exceptionally interesting (see Bullough 1975, pp. 334–9). It is just possible to cobble up a non-Bermuda-Pamphlets case, using the more fabulous Old World material, and Montaigne, while acknowledging that the name 'Setebos' comes from Patagonia, and Trinculo's 'dead Indian' [II.ii.33] and Miranda's 'brave new world' [v.i.182–3] could refer elsewhere, thus removing the colonialist interests from the play altogether: possible, but surely wrong. Admit such interests as influences on Shakespeare's play, and significance comes flooding in: and the colonialist loading, of play and pamphlets, whichever way round, becomes inescapable. Moreover, Shakespeare's play surely does suggest the customarily-listed New World interests (see Frey 1979).

5 Caliban

It is necessary to pause again, and look again at the complexity of Caliban and note in passing the discussion of some of the traditions said to have gone into the making of him (see Kermode, pp. xxxiii–xxxix, xlii; Lee 1929; Felperin 1962, p. 263; Bullough 1975, pp. 253–5; Orgel 1987, pp. 11, 15).

What Shakespeare made of him is another matter altogether. It was an eighteenth-century critic, Joseph Warton, who in his *Remarks on the Creation of Character* (1753) wrote:

Shakespeare seems to be the only poet who possesses the power of uniting poetry with propriety of character; of which I know not an instance more striking, than the image Calyban makes use of to express silence, which is at once highly poetical, and exactly suited to the wildness of the speaker:

> Pray you tread softly, that the blind mole may not
> Hear a foot-fall.

A. D. Nuttall notes:

Caliban, though horribly unchildlike, belongs to a world most of us have known as children. He lives in an intellectual half-light of bites, pinches, nettle-stings, terrors, cupboard-love, glimpses of extraordinary and inexplicable beauty. These things play a negligible part in the society of adults, but most of us remember a society in which they were intensely familiar. It was Caliban who, like a child, 'cried to dream again', was taught how to talk, and shown the Man in the Moon. The character of Caliban shows us objects which are too close to be seen in the ordinary way of things. His world is near-sighted, tactile, downward-looking, lacking in distant prospects. . . . The nature-poetry of the play (much of it Caliban's) is extremely interesting. It, too, is full of minute observations and gigantic distances, with a strange salt-sweetness hardly to be found elsewhere. We may skim the play, creaming off images which illustrate its special flavour – 'the ooze of the salt deep . . . the veins of the earth when it is baked with frost', 'unwholesome fen . . . berries . . . brine-pits', 'yellow sands . . . the wild waves whist', 'sea-water . . . fresh brook mussels, withered roots and husks, wherein the acorn cradles', 'bogs, fens, flats', 'a rock by the sea-side', 'show thee a jay's nest and instruct thee how To snare the nimble marmoset; I'll bring thee To clust'ring filberts, and sometimes I'll get thee Young scamels from the rock', 'Where crabs grow . . . pignuts', 'the quick freshes' (Nuttall 1967, pp. 140–1)

Caliban speaks, as we saw above (p. 46) some of the most beautiful poetry in the play. Indeed, in a note at III.ii.36–7, Kermode writes 'Caliban so often approaches verse as to provoke the suspicion that some passages at some stage have been deliberately broken down from verse to prose.' And of his last speech in the play, Anne Barton noted 'Caliban at least gets further than either Antonio or Sebastian in the direction of self-knowledge and understanding of the situation, although his primary achievement seems to be the recognition that his new masters were unworthy of respect' (Barton 1968, p. 177). Caliban, as Stephen Orgel implies, was thirteen when the two-year-old Miranda arrived on the island, and 'the two children have been educated together on the island, the objects of Prospero's devoted care' (Orgel 1987, p. 28).

I do not wish to sentimentalise Caliban: merely to enjoy a moment of Shakespeare's poetical calm before the twentieth-century political storm. For he is probably lying when he says 'this island's mine' – his mother was, as J. P. Brockbank puts it, 'a disreputable exile from Argier with only a casual claim to dominion over the island. Thus the play qualifies the righteousness of Caliban's resentment' (Brockbank 1966, p. 393).

Sympathy for Caliban has not been unfamiliar to theatre-goers, ever since Garrick in 1757 (when he restored Shakespeare's text to the stage in place of Davenant). Trevor R. Griffiths has traced the growth of Caliban in the theatre, passing through being an embodiment of republican and anti-slavery sentiments to get to his fuller role from 1871: malign, but less diabolical, more elementally human, at once more richly comic and more deeply tragic. Today he is a continually refractory presence (Griffiths 1983). Sir Sidney Lee pointed to his indispensability to Prospero, characteristic of the relation of Indian to planter (Lee 1929).

D. O. Mannoni, in a seminal book, first in French, *La Psychologie de la Colonisation* (1950), and then in English as *Prospero and Caliban* (1956), saw Caliban, as Jonathan Miller put it, as 'the demoralised, detribalised, dispossessed suffering field hand' (Miller 1970). From that point, a critical tradition began to assert strongly that Caliban's condition was Prospero's fault (see Greenblatt 1976). Prospero's attempts to educate Caliban and civilise him have only demoralised him completely. He is unable to learn even how to avoid suffering, and his idea of freedom is to attach himself at once to Stephano (and see Orgel 1987, pp. 23–5). His history comes to us through Prospero, how corrupted we can only guess: he wanted to 'people all the isle with Calibans' – the vicious punishment Prospero imposed says as much about his terror of the unregulated sensual, or of Yahoos threatening his rational rule, as it does about Caliban's bestial destructiveness. Ceres, whose fullness and ripeness is the centre of the betrothal, herself 'invokes a myth in which the crucial act of destruction is the rape of a daughter' (Orgel 1987, p. 49).

Michael Echeruo, the distinguished Nigerian scholar, wrote: 'many Caribbean, African and Black American writers have taken their cue from Caliban in regarding the rape of the Mirandas of this world as the only telling hurt they can inflict on the colonising or tyrannizing white man' (1980, p. xx). In recent Caribbean literature, Caliban appears steadily as a figure in relation to the white man. Aimé Césaire rewrote *The Tempest* in a West Indian plantation setting with Caliban at the centre. The same theme appears in Césaire's *Cahier*, in the work of Edouard Glissant and Leon Damas. The Caliban figure is prominent in Edward Braithwaite's *Islands*, and his other poetry and writing, and in Derek Walcott's play *Dream on Monkey Mountain*, in Vic Reid's *Leopards*, and the work of Austin Clarke, and Edgar Mittelholzer: and see C. L. R. James, *Black Jacobin*. Some of David Dabydeen's poems, especially in *Slave Song* (1984), and *Coolie Odyssey* (1988), explore the fantasied relation of modern black slave and white woman, set off by Caliban's desire for Miranda.

George Lamming's fifth novel, *Water with Berries* (1971), about West Indians in the U.K., has been described as 'Caliban in Albion'; it uses multiple levels of allegory, and is about the conflict between immigrant and native Briton, with Prospero, Caliban and three Caliban figures identifiable (see Paquet 1982). Lamming's *The Pleasures of Exile* (1960) has, as its sixth essay, 'A Master, A Child, A Slave'; this is specifically about the modern Caribbean experience of 'a state which is absolutely run by one man' who is sadistic to his slave, the Caliban, while the Ariel is elevated to be not a slave but a privileged servant, Prospero's source of information, 'the embodiment . . . of the perfect and unspeakable secret police' (Lamming 1960, p. 98). 'Caliban', he writes 'is a condition'. He notes the likeness of circumstance between Miranda and Caliban. 'Miranda has no recollection of her mother, like many an African slave' (p. 112). Caliban carried her on his back as a child. 'Prospero's imperialism is like an illness', not only in his personal relationships, but in his relation to the external and foreign world. . . . Sadism is characteristic of this type' (p. 113). In contrast to Prospero's memory of Miranda's mother, 'the memory of Sycorax, Caliban's mother, arouses him to rage that is almost insane . . . his mother was "a so-and-so"' (p. 115).

Lamming's account of some colonialist attitudes is, it must be said, uncomfortably accurate. He concludes, 'For the real sin [Prospero's] is not hatred, which implies involvement, but the calculated and habitual annihilation of the person whose presence you can ignore but never exclude'. Lamming describes 'the distance and purgatory which have always separated them [such Prosperos] from their forgotten slave' (p. 116).

6 Prospero

But Prospero is a Renaissance Mage, a theurgist, 'whose Art is to achieve supremacy over the natural world by holy magic' (Kermode 1964, p. xl). 'His Art is . . . the disciplined exercise of virtuous knowledge . . . a technique for liberating the soul from the passions . . . the practical application of a discipline of which the primary requirements are learning and temperance, and of which the mode is contemplation' (xlvii–xlviii). He sums up Shakespeare's life-long interest in magic: he is a magician like Rosalind's, 'most profound in his art and yet not damnable' [*As You Like It*, v.ii.60]. His magic is only 'rough' in that it is 'unsubtle by comparison with the next degree of the mage's enlightenment' (Kermode, p. 115; and see Sisson 1970; Yates 1975). Indeed, his benevolence can be made to be so cloying that he is in danger of standing on stage like one of Dickens's Cheeryble brothers in fancy-dress, presiding over rather energetic home theatricals. In one jump we seem to be a long way from the sadistic absolute ruler of black slaves, in modern Caribbean experience and fancy.

Yet it was his secret studies that set the whole discord and treason in motion. Recent critics find bad things in Prospero's magic: he is like Sycorax. 'Not only are their histories similar and their powers interchangeable, but both sorceress and magician are driven by the same passion – anger' (de Grazia 1981, p. 255; and see Orgel 1987, pp. 21–2, 25). If it is his magic which has taught him to be a good ruler on the island, it seems to have been the same magic which taught him to be a bad one in Milan. His control over Caliban's history, and over the latter's claim to the island, show him in a bad light. And we have to be reminded that it was Hazlitt, in the course of a lively attack printed in the radical *Yellow Dwarf* of

February 14, 1818, on Coleridge's current Shakespeare lectures, who first pointed out that 'Prospero and the rest are usurpers' (Hazlitt, 1934; p. 207).

One way out of the paradox is to say that Prospero is not a 'character' at all: 'He is scarcely a man in that way; he strikes one as being all mind' (Knight 1948, p. 232); I.ii is 'the tranquil discourse of two angelic beings who might have stepped out of Blake '(Nuttall 1967, p. 141). For others he is simply a Freudian case-history (Sundelson 1980). It is true that the jolt we experience coming from the great tragedies to the Romances is the sudden absence of revealed interior lives: but Prospero is on stage continually from III.iii on, and Shakespeare's confidence in his power to interest suggests something more than a pantomime wizard. Twentieth-century stagings have increasingly gone for a more ambiguous Prospero, particularly those productions that have not interfered with the ending, and have allowed the problem of the epilogue full weight. For, as Stephen Orgel says, 'Prospero's epilogue is unique in the Shakespeare canon in that its speaker declares himself not an actor in a play but a character in a fiction. The release he craves of the audience is the freedom to continue his history beyond the limits of the stage and text' (1987, p. 204).

Prospero in recent criticism has been 'a noble ruler and mage, a tyrant and megalomaniac, a necromancer, a Neoplatonic scientist, a colonial imperialist, a civilizer' (Orgel 1987, p. 11). Though it is Ariel who changes shape so easily, part of Prospero's magic may be that he can make himself look so various in the late twentieth century. And just as Caribbean writers have claimed Caliban from the Old World tyranny, so on the other side of the coin modern American critics find Prospero representing four centuries of the American soul (see Fiedler 1972; Frey 1979). Louis Marx, in the second chapter of his book *The Machine in the Garden: Technology and the Pastoral Ideal in America* (1964), finds the apparent glorification of the pastoral in *The Tempest* 'remarkably like the pattern of our typical American fables. . . . The topography of *The Tempest* anticipates the moral geography of the American imagination . . . the singular degree of plausibility that it attaches to the notion of a pastoral retreat' (p. 72). The most recent extension of using *The Tempest* in this way comes from the American critic Thomas Cartelli, who finds Prospero the model for brutal British colonialism in Africa, by means of a 'reading' of a novel by the Kenyan writer Ngugi Wa Thiong'o, *A Grain of Wheat* (1967). Cartelli imputes to George Lamming the idea of a Shakespeare who is 'a formative *producer* and *purveyor* of a paternalistic ideology that is basic to the material aims of western imperialism' (my italics) – which is not how I read Lamming, or Shakespeare. On top of what I myself feel are misreadings of *A Grain of Wheat* and Ngugi's essays in *Homecomings: Essays on Caribbean Literature, Culture and Politics* (1972) Cartelli builds a top-heavy and shaky structure whereby Prospero's paternalist colonialism includes Kurtz's corruption of it in Conrad's *Heart of Darkness*, Kurtz being 'a latent, potential or actualised version of Prospero': Cartelli is trying to examine 'Prospero's contribution to the development of colonialist discourse and behaviour' (Cartelli 1987, p. 104). He constructs a heavy case against Britain, and Shakespeare, using Lugard, Stanley, Rhodes and so on. The argument, however, is flawed. For one thing, Ngugi writes that Shakespeare *dramatised* not *caused* 'the practice and psychology of colonisation' (Ngugi 1972, p. 7): for another, Cartelli offers no other evidence. This is important. If the new American criticism of *The Tempest* is going to proceed in this way, we need to be alert to the fallacies. Cartelli's assertion that the play was an active contributor to the dark side of British involvement in Africa (though Stanley was an Amercian, of course) lacks all evidence, and mistakes discussion about colonialism (as far as a play can be a discussion) for its cause. At the time of the American Watergate crisis, there came from U.S. critics an unusually thick flurry of books and papers about Shakespeare's history plays, in which fundamental crises of nationhood were safely studied at several removes. Perhaps we are now to expect that American unease about foreign policy will lead to an increase in comment on *The Tempest* and the distant British in Africa. Already, the whole-sale Americanisation of *The Tempest* is a flourishing enterprise (Vaughan, 1988).

7   New 'readings'

The attempt to make Prospero and Caliban into polar opposites, with one – either one – as cause and the other as effect,
is always bound to be defeated in the end by Shakespeare.
To touch on the current fashionable insights, he deconstructs
such 'objective' polarity, allowing the reader to occupy the
space. Much very modern criticism in this area is so densely
written as to be fairly impenetrable, which is a pity. Francis
Barker and Peter Hulme try to be open to many 'readings' of
The Tempest, identifying 'in all texts a potential for new linkages
to be made and thus for new political meanings to be
constructed' (Barker and Hulme 1985, p. 193) and rejecting
both 'politicised intertextuality' and 'the autotelic text', with
its single fixed meaning. By means of the theory of discourse,
and focusing on the themes of legitimacy and usurpation, they
are able to examine two plays, *The Tempest* and 'Prospero's
play', which is not quite the same thing. Prospero imposes his
construction of events on the others. When Caliban accuses
Prospero of usurping the island [I.ii.333–4] Prospero's

> sole – somewhat hysterical – response consists of an indirect denial
> ('Thou most lying slave' [I.ii.346]) and a counter accusation of attempted
> rape ('thou didst seek to violate / The honour of my child' [I.ii.349–50]),
> which together foreclose the exchange and serve in practice as Prospero's
> only justification for the arbitrary rule he exercises over the island and
> its inhabitants. At a stroke he erases from what we have called Prospero's
> play all trace of the moment of his reduction of Caliban to slavery and
> appropriation of his island. . . . But, despite his evasiveness, this moment
> ought to be of decisive *narrative* importance since it marks Prospero's self-
> installation as ruler, and his acquisition, through Caliban's enslavement,
> of the means of supplying the food and labour on which he and Miranda
> are completely dependent. . . . Through its very occlusion of Caliban's
> version of proper beginnings, Prospero's disavowal is itself performative
> of the discourse of colonialism, since this particular reticulation of denial
> of dispossession with retrospective justification for it, is the characteristic
> trope by which European colonial regimes articulated their authority
> over land to which they could have no conceivable legitimate claim. . . .
> The success of this trope is, as so often in these cases, proved by its
> subsequent invisibility.   (p. 200)

By way of a neat, brief, discussion of the convolutions of the
word 'treachery' in relation to comments on both *The Tempest*
and the natives, Barker and Hulme arrive at their strong

point: 'Colonialist legitimation has always had then to go on to tell its own story, inevitably one of native violence: Prospero's play performs this task within *The Tempest*' (p. 201). What follows has the satisfying sound of bolts going home:

> The burden of Prospero's play is already deeply concerned with producing legitimacy. The purpose of Prospero's main plot is to secure recognition of his claim to the usurped duchy of Milan, a recognition sealed in the blessing given by Alonso to the prospective marriage of his own son to Prospero's daughter. As part of this, Prospero reduces Caliban to a role in the supporting sub-plot, as instigator of a mutiny that is programmed to fail, thereby forging an equivalence between Antonio's initial *putsch* and Caliban's revolt. This allows Prospero to annul the memory of his failure to prevent his expulsion from the dukedom, by repeating it as a mutiny that he will, this time, forestall. But, in addition, the playing out of the colonialist narrative is thereby completed: Caliban's attempt – tarred with the brush of Antonio's supposedly self-evident viciousness – is produced as final and irrevocable confirmation of the natural treachery of savages. (p. 201)

The main plot of Prospero's play runs according to plan, but 'the sub-plot produces the only real moment of drama when Prospero calls a sudden halt to the celebratory masque'. They add 'One way of distinguishing Prospero's play from *The Tempest* might be to claim that Prospero's carefully established relationship between main and sub-plot is reversed in *The Tempest*, whose *main* plot concerns Prospero's anxiety over his *sub*-plot' (p. 203).

As I write, the universe of *The Tempest* has never been bigger: critical models have to be more than three-dimensional. Now the very repressions themselves reflected in the play are to be viewed from a quite different, fourth, plane. The reader, moreover, sits in a fifth plane and responds (to put it crudely) according to what he had for breakfast (dyspeptically, if his breakfast was on the plane).

An example of the deconstructive work which is now the norm would show the simultaneous acknowledgement both that it was Freud who first drew the analogy between the political operations of colonialism and the modes of psychic repression; and the passionate denial of having any truck whatsoever with Freudianism's 'a-historical, Europocentric and sexist models of psychical development'. This disclaimer comes in the lengthy notes to an article on *The Tempest* by Paul Brown (1985), with acknowledgement to Stephen Greenblatt (1980). Brown's analysis of the play is dense and difficult, revealing, as far as I understand it, sets of central ambivalences in the narrative.

> At the 'close' of the play, Prospero is in danger of becoming the other to the narrative declaration of his own project, which is precisely the ambivalent position Caliban occupies. *The Tempest*, then, declares no all-embracing triumph for colonialism. Rather it serves as a limit text in which the characteristic operations of colonialist discourse may be discerned – as an instrument of exploitation, a register of beleaguerment and a site of radical ambivalence. These operations produce strategies and stereotypes which seek to impose and efface colonialist power; in this text they are also driven into contradiction and disruption. The play's 'ending' in renunciation and restoration is only the final ambivalence, being at once the apotheosis, mystification and potential erosion of the colonialist discourse. If this powerful discourse, thus mediated, is finally reduced to the stuff of dreams, then it is still dream work, the site of a struggle for meaning.   (pp. 68–9)

Part Two
Appraisal

The courtly *Tempest*

THE SPECIALNESS OF *The Tempest* – something like a court masque, but altogether firmer, less evanescent – would have been seen by James I and its first audiences to have been in that very open-ness we are just learning to celebrate again: its meanings both firmly rooted, as in its celebration of royal power in the new plantation in James Town, Virginia; and at the same time free to change shapes at the behest of the royal master: to have, by good magic, freedom in space and time. *The Tempest* is indeed a play which, though firmly established in the very front of the 1623 Folio, has continued a free life, successively turning into new shapes of great interest, from Milton's *Comus* to Auden's *The Sea and the Mirror*, from Fletcher to the late-twentieth-century Caribbean remakings. Other plays have been adapted: only *The Tempest* lives on in quite this remarkable way.

The triumphal arrival of James as monarch in March 1604 established a great change in courtly, and civic, aesthetic in London. The fearful, cynical atmosphere of the last years of Elizabeth was to be banished: triumphal arches set the tone of spectacular, decorative, romantic exuberance. Poets, playwrights, designers, painters, musicians and choreographers were encouraged to make spectacles, and suddenly found that they had court money and court status with which to work. Shakespeare's company became The King's Men.

Shakespeare's most courtly early play, *Love's Labour's Lost*, was revived in 1604. Some years later, possibly after revising *King Lear* for the Blackfriars in 1608 (again possibly, our Folio version), he stopped writing towering transcendencies about heroes in tragic dilemmas, moved away even from the popular

85

theatre of *Pericles* (which Jonson called a 'mouldy tale'), and adopted the new neo-classical interests. Instead of the now apparently unfashionable developed inner life of a Hamlet or Othello or Macbeth, he gave his audiences networks of significance, developments of those arts of perspective which were newly coming in from Europe, fresh ways of seeing which included *genera mixta* like tragicomedy.

I suppose that the nearest to a complete system of correspondences that we can think of is a court at home in a city, though even that, of course, is not perfect, and involves holding tensions in a difficult balance. The neo-classical values, 'Augustan' in their reference both to Emperor and Rome, are urban, urbane even, civil, 'civilised' if that means, as Aristotle held, keeping barbarism at bay. Shakespeare's last city play had been *Coriolanus*, where the vividly-realised Rome was torn apart with a great wound in its central nervous system, only healed by one man's sacrifice, saving the city from destruction. In the unfinished play just before, Timon had abandoned Athens, betrayed by civil corruption into misanthropy. *The Tempest* is about establishing values in a New World: the court is now sailing away for a fresh beginning, having been on a sinking ship in which passengers and crew were, like nature, violently at odds. However full of nature-images and natural forces the play is, Gonzalo's outburst of joy at the transformations just revealed to the royal party is very much in terms of the monumental buildings and decoration of a new city court – he wants it 'set down/With gold on lasting pillars':

> Was Milan thrust from Milan, that his issue
> Should become Kings of Naples? O, rejoice
> Beyond a common joy! and set it down
> With gold on lasting pillars: in one voyage
> Did Claribel her husband find at Tunis,
> And Ferdinand, her brother, found a wife
> Where he himself was lost, Prospero his dukedom
> In a poor isle, and all of us ourselves
> When no man was his own.

> [v.i.205–13]

His joy is dynastic – the right fathers and children will rule from inside those 'lasting pillars'. A new Golden Age will come.

This courtly complexity is, I believe, the real significance of the networks of correspondences we began to explore above in Part One. Shakespeare chose not to go Jonson's way and create lavish masques for the court, packed with every conceivable method of stating meaning. In several ways that is a relief. Anyone who has studied how Jonson *published*, as opposed to staged, his masques (*Hymenaei* makes a convenient example) is surely staggered by both the weight of meaning expounded in the learnedly chattering margins and at the foot of every page, crowding the main text into a corner with Latin, Greek and Italian references, abbreviations, and expositions: and also by the fact that Jonson had rather desperately to do that to get his meaning across. Further, unless properly trained we are blind to the significance of Jonson's precious numbers, on which so much of the choreography of a masque like *Hymenaei* depends. *The Tempest* simply stands, bare of annotation, at the front of a volume of plays. On the other hand, however, we are undoubtedly missing something important. The constellations of internal correspondencies are probably linked to others we have not yet woken up to. Though a recent attempt to find the court performance of *The Tempest* on All Saints Day (Hallowmass) full of meaning from the Christian calendar (Bender 1980) depended in the end on too many conjectures and unprovable assumptions, as yet unpublished work by John Orrell on the numerology in *The Winter's Tale* (communicated privately) does point both to a remarkably full-blooded number system in that play, and its significance in relation to the Christian year.

The courtly context for *The Tempest* is international. Jonson, and Inigo Jones especially, looked abroad to Europe. Even James's Scottish court had been more French in aesthetic outlook than we have been ready to see. Shakespeare in London was not England's National Poet if that means cutting England off at Dover – or a few yards further south of the Thames. We make a great mistake if we deny him his awareness of the full flood of European thinking in many significant areas, from the high Genevan Calvinism visible in *Hamlet* for example, to the Italian neo-Platonism of a play like *Antony and Cleopatra*. And when Shakespeare was in mid-career, new methods of stage effect were arriving in London from the Continent; as well as wonderfully expressive costumes, there were effects that fed perspective, like movable scenery and cleverer lighting effects – all that grand flowing sweep of spectacle that we label Baroque. The lavishness of the Italian and French courts was infecting the English. There was much traffic, both ways. Again, we forget how many of London's actors, including some from Shakespeare's company, penetrated deeply into Europe.

The courtly context for *The Tempest* is international: and that includes the New World. London was for Spenser in *The Faerie Queene*, and for others, New Troy. Aeneas, leaving old Troy to found a new city, crossed the Mediterranean north from Carthage (which is Tunis, says Gonzalo) on precisely the route taken by Alonso's party going home after Claribel's wedding. In Shakespeare's 'sources', Sir John Gates was on his way, like an Aeneas again, to the newly-being-founded James Town in Virginia. A recent study (Gillies 1986) shows the importance of the Virginian context for understanding *The Tempest*: the two key motifs that he sees in the play and its 'sources', temperance and fruitfulness, are, he says, both Virginian and Ovidian. The sources, like the play, are a construct of classical responses (and see Wiltenburg 1987).

Perhaps after all *The Tempest* should have had Jonsonian notes smothering the page with terrifying erudition (though who could possibly match Jonson? the reader thinks: a reaction which Jonson must have anticipated). Or perhaps not. All we have is a play. Who now reads the printed *Hymenaei*? Who even knows where to find it? Every Desert Island castaway, equipped by the BBC with Bible and Shakespeare, has *The Tempest*. That apparently infinite interacting system of relationships goes on living. The distance that *The Tempest* covers is not just geographic. Somewhere in those hidden and undeclared charges of meaning are continued creative energies.

The first great offshoot, as is well known, was Milton's *Comus* (1634): before and after that, the seventeenth-century adaptations, though felt to be of little comparative value today, had in them something perhaps just a little better than cooperative butchery. Unusually, however, *The Tempest*'s life extends well outside drama. To give a few examples, more or less at random: *Robinson Crusoe* (1719) is *The Tempest*-as-novel-

of-its-time. Shelley's 'With a Guitar, to Jane', is as if from
Ariel to Miranda. Browning's 'Caliban upon Setebos' is a rich
dramatic monologue in which Caliban muses on his god.
Ernst Rénan, of *Vie de Jésus* fame (or notoriety), wrote
a sequel to the play (*Caliban*, 1878) 'adaptées aux idées de
notre temps', with Ariel as idealism, Prospero as aristocratic
man and Caliban, democracy. *The Tempest* haunts T. S. Eliot's
The Waste Land, is echoed in Beckett's *Waiting for Godot*, and
stimulated Henry James to a great critical introduction written
when he was sixty-four, in which he expresses his bafflement at
Shakespeare stopping writing at forty-six. As Philip Edwards
summed up,

> He is led on to think of the total inscrutability of Shakespeare the man,
> and feels that he is never nearer to Shakespeare than when, having
> shown in *The Tempest* quite a new power and energy, freed from every
> compromise and sacrifice he has formerly had to make, and at last totally
> dedicated to his art – he commits the finally incomprehensible gesture
> of giving up writing   [Edwards 1973, p. 123]

The play has been the subject of a seminal critical edition,
Frank Kermode's Arden, and at the other end of the spectrum,
a startlingly original film by Derek Jarman – the Hollywood
Forbidden Planet was something different again. Sir Michael
Tippett's *The Knot Garden* (1970) is another operatic relation
of *The Tempest*. Some of the modern Caribbean work we have
already briefly discussed (above, pp. 78–9). Harry Mulisch's
Dutch novel, translated by Adrienne Dixon as *Last Call* (1987)
has performances of the play woven into its complex structure.
The most important modern offshoot is Auden's 'The Sea and
the Mirror', written between 1942 and 1944, and published
in *For the Time Being*. Here the stage manager addresses
the critics; Prospero says farewell to Ariel; and then 'The
Supporting Cast, Sotto Voce', imagined *en route* back to Naples,
speak in turn, in verses of brilliance and considerable insight.
In the last long section, Caliban speaks, somewhat bafflingly,
a pastiche of Henry James, 'To the Audience', on the subject
of the relation of Art and Life. Finally, Ariel speaks a
'Postscript' to Caliban. (Some of these works, and a few others
of the many that there are, are discussed by Ruby Cohn in
her *Modern Shakespeare Offshoots*, 1976.) I add that it is striking

that the dominant figure in so many that I have seen is
Caliban.

Anne Barton writes:

> There is a sense in which *The Tempest* is a kind of latter-day myth. Like
> the story of Oedipus, of Iphigenia, or of Prometheus, the events which
> occur on Prospero's island possess a meaning at once irreducible and
> mysterious. They demand interpretation and expansion. The difference,
> of course, lies in the fact that nothing derived from *The Tempest* is anything
> like as great or as satisfying as it.   (1968, p. 20)

The Tempest is apparently limitless in its productive power.
Perhaps if we read it right, it will tell us more about the
Shakespearean process, too. Does it stand first because it
points a way to read all Shakespeare?

Whatever it is, and however mysteriously it works, we must
be grateful that it stands there in print, and was not, like
Jonsonian masque, cancellable. Gary Schmidgall refers to a
masque of 1613:

> James, weary of all the festivities, had 'no edge to it' and he cancelled
> the performance. Chamberlain wrote afterward in a letter of both the
> novelty and ephemerality of the masque: 'But the grace of the Mask is
> quite gone, when their apparel hath been already showed, and their
> devises vented, so that how it will fall out God knows; for they [the
> producers] are much discouraged and out of countenance'. Masques
> were for one time only.   (1981, p. 136)

Though Prospero says that his insubstantial pageant leaves
not a rack behind, *The Tempest* endures. It depends on
metaphor not machinery; the magical transformations are not
in rumbling stage devices but in the language, and therefore
transmittable, regardless of royal mood. If we come to the
Complete Shakespeare expecting transformation, then we
shall find it. The Folio is a 'popular' volume, its readership
not limited to the court. *The Tempest* might well be setting a
context in which all the plays in the book can be read by
anybody. True, Prospero and Caliban have their contemporary significances, traditional and political, as well as being
especially original. But, while revolving round each other, as
we saw above, they also have a sort of floating free life,
deconstructed from any fixed system. They have, as Prospero's

Epilogue to the play shows, and as Auden suggests, a new fictional, indeed mythical, energy.

After the ordeal by tempest, the voyagers found a new union in the island inheritance. The Bermuda Pamphlets as well as *The Tempest* demonstrate how survivors have to be saved from each other. This cold douche of reality is Shakespeare's contribution to the world of theatrical illusion, whether that was in Jonson's masques, or in a play of pseudo-wizardry like his *Alchemist* (presented by Shakespeare's company at the same time as *The Tempest*, with interesting implications). Alonso, the keystone of the arch of the new union, sails away with his company to start afresh; not by any means perfectly – Antonio and Sebastian, as Auden brings out, are still up to something; Ariel has gone; Caliban is left behind. But the union, like that new one of Scotland with England, is firm enough to warrant Gonzalo's benediction.

The Tempest should, like the ceiling of that Banqueting House in Whitehall where it was first performed, be a monument to a new sense of certainty. The play stands at the front of its great volume just as Genesis opens that other handsome Folio being put together by scholars and others, under King James's direction, and coming off the press at the time of the same royal impulse to classicise: and both have had an extraordinarily influential life.

References

NOTE: here and in the text dates of publication are those of the edition cited, not necessarily those of the first edition.

Armstrong, E. A., *Shakespeare's Imagination* (London, 1946).

Aronson, Alex, *Psyche & Symbol in Shakespeare* (Indiana, 1972).

Barker, Francis and Hulme, Peter, 'Nymphs and reapers heavily vanish: the discursive con-texts of *The Tempest*', in Drakakis (1985).

Barton, Anne, *The New Penguin Shakespeare: The Tempest* (Harmondsworth, 1968).

Bate, Jonathan, *Shakespeare and the English Romantic Imagination* (Oxford, 1986).

Beer, Gillian, *The Romance* (London, 1970).

Bender, John B., 'The Day of *The Tempest*', *English Literary History* (1980).

Bentley, G. E., 'Shakespeare and the Blackfriars Theatre', *Shakespeare Survey*, 1 (1948) 38–50.

Binns, J. W., 'Shakespeare's Latin Citations: the Editorial Problem', *Shakespeare Survey*, 35 (1982) 119–28.

Boughner, Daniel C., 'Jonsonian Structure in *The Tempest*', *Shakespeare Quarterly*, 21 (1970) 3–10.

Brockbank, J. Philip, '*The Tempest*: Conventions of Art and Empire' in Brown and Harris (1966); reprinted in Palmer (1971).

Brower, Reuben A., 'The Mirror of Analogy: *The Tempest*' in *The Fields of Light: An Experiment in Critical Reading* (New York, 1951); reprinted in Palmer (1968) and Palmer (1971).

Brown, John Russell, 'Three Adaptations', *Shakespeare Survey*, 13 (1960) 137–45.

Brown, John Russell, *Shakespeare: The Tempest* (London, 1969).

Brown, John Russell, and Harris, Bernard (eds), *Later Shakespeare*. Stratford-upon-Avon Studies, 8 (London, 1966).

Brown, Paul, 'This thing of darkness I acknowledge mine: *The Tempest* and the discourse of colonialism' in Dollimore and Sinfield (1985).

Bullough, Geoffrey, *Narrative and Dramatic Sources of Shakespeare*, VIII (London, 1975).

Cartelli, Thomas, 'Prospero in Africa' in Howard and O'Connor (1987).

Césaire, Aimé, *Cahier* (Paris, 1960).

Césaire, Aimé, Une Tempête (Paris, 1969).

Chambers, E. K., *Shakespeare: A Survey* (London, 1925).

Chambers, E. K., *William Shakespeare: A Study of Facts and Problems* (Oxford, 1930).

Chambers, E. K., *Shakespearean Gleanings* (London, 1944).

Clemen, W. H., *The Development of Shakespeare's Imagery* (London, 1951).

Cody, Richard, *The Landscape of the Mind* (Oxford, 1969).

Cohn, Ruby, *Modern Shakespeare Offshoots* (Princeton, 1976).

Colie, Rosalie, *Resources of Kind: Genre-Theory in the Renaissance* (Berkeley, 1973).

Crow, John, 'Deadly Sins of Criticism, or, Seven Ways to Get Shakespeare Wrong' in *Shakespeare Quarterly*, 9 (1958) 301–5.

Dabydeen, David, *Slave Song* (Coventry, 1984).

Dabydeen, David, *Coolie Odyssey* (Coventry, 1988).

Dean, John, *Restless Wanderers: Shakespeare and the Pattern of Romance* (Salzburg, 1979).

Dobrée, Bonamy, 'The Tempest' in *Essays and Studies NS*, v (1952), 13–25.

Doebler, John, *Shakespeare's Speaking Pictures: Studies in Iconic Imagery* (Albuquerque, 1974).

Dollimore, Jonathan and Sinfield, Alan (eds), *Political Shakespeare: New Essays in Cultural Materialism* (Manchester, 1985).

Dowden, Edward, *Shakspere – his Mind and Art* (London, 1875).

Drakakis, John (ed.), *Alternative Shakespeares* (London, 1985).

Echeruo, Michael (ed.), *Shakespeare: The Tempest*, New Swan Shakespeare: Advanced Series (London, 1980).

Edwards, Philip, 'Shakespeare's Romances: 1900–1957', *Shakespeare Survey*, 11 (1958) 1–18.

Edwards, Philip, 'The Late Comedies' in *Shakespeare: Select Bibliographical Guides*, ed. Stanley Wells (Oxford, 1973).

Ellis-Fermor, Una, *The Jacobean Drama* (London, 1936).

Felperin, Howard, *Shakespearean Romance* (Princeton, 1972).

Fiedler, Leslie A., *The Stranger in Shakespeare* (New York, 1972).

Fineman, Joel, 'Fratricide and Cuckoldry: Shakespeare's Doubles' in Schwartz and Kahn (1980).

Foakes, R. A., *Shakespeare, The Dark Comedies to the Last Plays: From Satire to Celebration* (London, 1971).

Forman, Maurice Buxton (ed.), *The Letters of John Keats* (Oxford, 1947).

Frey, Charles, '*The Tempest* and the New World', *Shakespeare Quarterly*, 30 (1979), pp. 29–41.

Frye, Northrop, *A Natural Perspective: The Development of Shakespearean Comedy and Romance* (London, 1965).

Frye, Northrop, 'The Argument of Comedy', *English Institute Essays* 1948 (1949 pp. 58–73; reprinted in Laurence Lerner (ed.), *Shakespeare's Comedies: An Anthology of Modern Criticism* (Harmondsworth, 1967).

Gesner, Carol, *Shakespeare and the Greek Romance: A Study of Origins* (Lexington, 1970).

Gillies, John, 'Shakespeare's Virginian Masque', *English Literary History*, 53 (1986) 673–707.

de Grazia, Margreta, '*The Tempest*: Gratuitous Movement or Action Without Kibes', *Shakespeare Studies*, 14 (1981).

Greenblatt, Stephen, 'Leaning to Curse: Aspects of Linguistic Colonialism in the Sixteenth Century' in Fredi Chiappelli (ed.) *First Images of America: The Impact of the New World on the Old* (Berkeley, 1976).

Greenblatt, Stephen, *Renaissance Self-Fashioning from More to Shakespeare* (Chicago, 1980).

Griffiths, Trevor R., ' "This Island's Mine": Caliban and Colonialism' in C. J. Rawson and G. K. Hunter (eds), *Yearbook of English Studies*, 13 (1983).

Grudin, Robert, 'Prospero's Masque and the Structure of *The Tempest*', *South Atlantic Quarterly*, 71 (1972) 401–9.

Hazlitt, William, *The Complete Works*, ed. P. P. Howe: vol. 19, *Literary and Political Criticism* (London, 1934).

Hillman, Richard, '*The Tempest* as Romance and Anti-Romance', *University of Toronto Quarterly*, 56 (1986).

Hirst, David L., *Tragicomedy* (London, 1984).

Hirst, David L., *The Tempest: Text and Performance* (London, 1984).

Holland, Norman N., *The Shakespearean Imagination* (London, 1964).

Holland, Norman N., *Psychoanalysis and Shakespeare* (New York, 1966).

Howard, Jean E. and O'Connor, Marion F., *Shakespeare Reproduced: the Text in History and Ideology* (London, 1987).

Hunter, R. G., *Shakespeare and the Comedy of Forgiveness* (New York, 1965).

James, D. G., *The Dream of Prospero* (Oxford, 1967).

Kahn, Coppélia, 'The Providential Tempest and the Shakespearean Family' in Schwartz and Kahn (1980).

Kastan, David Scott, "More Than History Can Pattern": Notes towards an Understanding of Shapespeare's Romances', *Cithara*, 17 (1977) 29–44.

Kermode, Frank, *The Tempest*, The Arden Shakespeare (London, 1964).

Knight, G. Wilson, *The Crown of Life* (London, 1948).

Knox, Bernard, *The Tempest* and the Ancient Comic Tradition', English Institute Essays 1954 (1955) pp. 52–73.

Kott, Jan, 'Prospero's Staff' in *Shakespeare Our Contemporary* (London, 1965); reprinted in Palmer (1968).

Lamming, George, *The Pleasures of Exile* (London, 1960).

Lea, K. M., *Italian Popular Comedy* (1934).

Lee, Sidney, 'The American Indian in Elizabethan England' in F. S. Boas (ed.), *Elizabethan and Other Essays* (1929).

Levin, Harry, 'Two Magian comedies: *The Tempest* and *The Alchemist*', *Shakespeare Survey*, 22 (1969) 47–58.

Levin, Richard, *New Readings vs. Old Plays* (Chicago, 1979).

Lindley, David (ed.), *The Court Masque* (Manchester, 1984).

Loughrey, Brian, and Taylor, Neil, 'Ferdinand and Miranda at Chess', *Shakespeare Survey*, 35 (1982) 113–18.

Mannoni, O., *Psychologie de la Colonisation* (Paris, 1950): translated by P. Powesland as *Prospero and Caliban: The Psychology of Colonisation* (New York, 1964).

Marienstras, Richard, translated by Janet Lloyd, *New Perspectives in the Shakespearean World* (Cambridge, 1985).

Marx, Leo, *The Machine in the Garden: Technology and the Pastoral Ideal in America* (New York, 1964).

Maus, Katharine Eisaman, 'Arcadia Lost: Politics and Revision in the Restoration *Tempest*', *Renaissance Drama*, N.S. 13 (1982) 198–209.

McFarland, Thomas, *Shakespeare's Pastoral Comedy* (Chapel Hill, 1972).

Mehl, Dieter, 'Emblematic Theatre', *Anglia*, 95 (1977) 130–8.

Melchiori, Barbara, 'Still Harping on My Daughter', *English Miscellany*, 11 (Rome, 1960) 59–74.

Miller, Jonathan, in Ralph Berry (ed.) *On Directing Shakespeare* (London, 1970).

Milward, Peter, *Shakespeare's Religious Background* (Bloomington, 1973).

Mulisch, Harry, translated by Adrienne Dixon, *Last Call* (London, 1987).

Ngugi, James (Ngugi Wa Thiong'o), *A Grain of Wheat* (London, 1967).

Ngugi, James (Ngugi Wa Thiong'o), *Homecomings: Essays on Caribbean Literature, Culture and Politics* (London, 1972).

Nuttall, A. D., *Two Concepts of Allegory* (London, 1967).

Orgel, Stephen, 'New Uses of Adversity: *Tragic Experience in The Tempest*' in Reuben A. Brower and Richard Poirier (eds), *in Defense of Reading*: A Reader's Approach to Literary Criticism (New York, 1962).

Orgel, Stephen, 'Prospero's Wife', *Representations*, 8 (1984) 1–13.

Orgel, Stephen, *The Oxford Shakespeare: The Tempest* (Oxford, 1987).

Orrell, John, 'The Musical Canon of Proportion in Jonson's *Hymenaei*', *English Language Notes*, 15 (1978).

Palmer, D. J. (ed.), *Shakespeare: The Tempest. A Casebook* (London, 1968).

Palmer, D. J. (ed.), *Shakespeare's Later Comedies: An Anthology of Modern Criticism* (Harmondsworth, 1971).

Paquet, Sandra Pouchet, *The Novels of George Lamming* (London, 1982).

Pettet, E. C., *Shakespeare and the Romance Tradition* (London, 1949).

Powell, Jocelyn, *Restoration Theatre Production* (London, 1984).

Proudfoot, Richard, 'Shakespeare and the New Dramatists of the King's Men, 1606–1613' in Brown and Harris (1966).

Raysor, T. M. (ed.) *Samuel Taylor Coleridge: Shakespearean Criticism* (2nd edn, 2 vols, London, 1960).

Schmidgall, Gary, *Shakespeare and the Courtly Aesthetic* (Berkeley, 1981).

Schwartz, Murray M. and Kahn, Coppélia, *Representing Shakespeare: New Psychoanalytic Essays* (Baltimore, 1980).

Seltzer, Daniel, 'The Staging of the Last Plays' in Brown and Harris (1966).

Sisson, C. J., 'The Magic of Prospero' in *Shakespeare Survey*, 11 (1970) 70–7.

Slater, Ann Pasternak, *Shakespeare the Director* (Brighton, 1982).

Spurgeon, Caroline, *Shakespeare's Imagery and What It Tells Us* (Cambridge, 1935).

Srigley, Michael, *Images of Regeneration. A Study of Shakespeare's 'The Tempest' and its Cultural Background* (Uppsala, 1985).

Still, Colin, *The Timeless Theme* (London, 1936).

Stoll, E. E., 'Certain Fallacies and Irrelevancies in the Literary Scholarship of the Day', *Studies in Philology*, 24 (1927).

Strachey, Lytton, 'Shakespeare's Final Period' in *Books and Characters, French and English* (London, 1922).

Sturgess, Keith, *Jacobean Private Theatre* (London, 1987).

Sundelson, David, 'So Rare a Wonder'd Father' in Schwartz and Kahn (1980).

Tillyard, E. M. W., *Shakespeare's Last Plays* (London, 1938).

Traversi, Derek, *Shakespeare: The Last Phase* (London, 1954).

Vaughan, Alden T., 'Shakespeare's Indian: The Americanization of Caliban', *Shakespeare Quarterly*, 39 (1988).

Wells, Stanley, 'Shakespeare and Romance' in Brown and Harris (1966); reprinted in Palmer (1971).

Welsford, Enid, *The Court Masque* (London, 1927).

White, R. S., *'Let wonder seem familiar': Endings in Shakespeare's romance vision* (London, 1985).

William, David *'The Tempest* on the Stage' in John Russell Brown and Bernard Harris (eds), *Jacobean Theatre*, Stratford-upon-Avon Studies, 1 (London, 1960); reprinted in Palmer (1971).

Wiltenburg, Robert, 'The Aeneid' in 'The Tempest', *Shakespeare Survey*, 39 (1987) 159–68.

Wright, Rosemary, 'Prospero's Lime Tree and the Pursuit of *Vanitas'*, *Shakespeare Survey*, 37 (1984) 133–40.

Yates, Frances A., *Shakespeare's Last Plays: A New Approach* (London, 1975).

Young, David, *The Heart's Forest: A Study of Shakespeare's Pastoral Plays* (New Haven, 1972).

Index